GCSE M[...]
Revision Guide

EDEXCEL

Alan Charlton

RHINEGOLD
EDUCATION

www.rhinegoldeducation.co.uk

Music Study Guides
GCSE, AS and A2 Music Study Guides (AQA, Edexcel and OCR)
GCSE, AS and A2 Music Listening Tests (AQA, Edexcel and OCR)
AS/A2 Music Technology Study Guide (Edexcel)
AS/A2 Music Technology Listening Tests (Edexcel)
Revision Guides for GCSE (AQA, Edexcel and OCR), AS and A2 Music (Edexcel)

Other Rhinegold Study Guides
Rhinegold publishes resources for candidates studying Drama and Theatre Studies

Also available from Rhinegold Education
Key Stage 3 Listening Tests: Book 1 and Book 2
AS and A2 Music Harmony Workbooks
GCSE and AS Music Composition Workbooks
GCSE and AS Music Literacy Workbooks
Romanticism in Focus, Baroque Music in Focus, Modernism in Focus, *The Immaculate Collection* in Focus,
Who's Next in Focus, *Batman* in Focus, *Goldfinger* in Focus, Musicals in Focus
Music Technology from Scratch, Dictionary of Music in Sound

First published 2010 in Great Britain by
Rhinegold Education
14–15 Berners Street
London W1T 3LJ
www.rhinegoldeducation.co.uk

© 2010 Rhinegold Education
a division of Music Sales Limited

Second impression 2011

You should always check the current requirements of the examination, since these may change.
Copies of the Edexcel specification can be downloaded from the Edexcel website at www.edexcel.com
Telephone: 01623 467467   Email: publications@linney.com

Edexcel GCSE Music Revision Guide
British Library Cataloguing in Publication Data.
A catalogue record for this book is available from the British Library.
Order No. RHG327
ISBN 978-1-907447-09-9
Printed in the EU

Contents

The author

Alan Charlton is a composer, writer, examiner and teacher. He holds a PhD in Composition from Bristol University and was the first Eileen Norris Fellow in Composition at Bedford School. A winner of many national and international awards for composition, performers of his music include The Lindsays and Birmingham Contemporary Music Group. He was Head of Music Technology at Bedford School for four years and is also an experienced Edexcel examiner and teacher of GCSE and A-level music. He has written and contributed to many books and study guides on music and is a regular writer for *Classroom Music* magazine.

Acknowledgements

The author would like to thank the consultant Paul Terry and the Rhinegold editorial and design team of Harriet Power and Reema Patel for their expert support in the preparation of this book.

Introduction

This guide is intended to help you through your Edexcel GCSE Listening and Appraising exam (Unit 3) which you take at the end of your Edexcel GCSE Music course. Before you begin, do double check that you are actually following the **Edexcel** specification and not OCR or AQA.

In this guide there are helpful **revision tips**, sections on each of the twelve **set works**, a revision of the **elements of music** and a **glossary** of musical terms used in the book. It is best to plan your revision first using the revision tips before moving on to the rest of the book.

The Edexcel exam is in **two sections**, both of which are based on the set works. The **first** section (lasting 65 minutes) is based around recorded excerpts of the set works and involves mostly short answers, while the **second** (lasting 25 minutes) doesn't use recordings and will require more extended writing. While you will be able to answer some questions using your general musical knowledge, for success in the exam you will need to **memorise facts and musical features** about each of the twelve set works. All of the information you need to know is covered in this guide, and there are questions on each work to help you with your revision. The answers to these may be found at www.rhinegoldeducation.co.uk. A guide to the sort of questions you are likely to be asked in the exam is included in the **elements of music** chapter.

When revising, try to set yourself frequent written tests and essay writing practice. Also make sure you **listen** to the set works regularly, with and without the score: your aural knowledge of the set works will be tested in the first section of the exam and it will be much easier to recall facts if you know them well.

Finally, try to combine this guide with some practice listening papers. This will help you to see how the information contained in this guide might be tested in an exam. There are more details on getting hold of practice papers in the revision tips section. Good luck!

Top ten revision tips

1. PLAN YOUR REVISION

Start revising as soon as you can, using the Christmas and Easter holidays if possible. The earlier you start preparing, the happier and more confident you will be in the weeks leading up to the exam.

First **devise a rough**, **overall plan**, deciding how much time you're going to spend on GCSE Music and, within that, how much time you're going to allocate to each topic. The most effective approach is to tackle the topics you are **least confident** about first, leaving your strengths until last. Include 'rest days' to avoid becoming jaded, and some 'general revision days' to give yourself some extra time if you need to catch up or cover a topic in more detail.

EXAMPLE 1

Time left: 16 days. Need to cover 12 topics. One topic per day = 12 days, plus 2 rest days, plus 2 days of general revision.

- Monday: Symphony No. 40
- Tuesday: *Rag Desh*
- Wednesday: 'Peripetie'
- Etc.

EXAMPLE 2

Time left: 31 days. Need to cover 12 topics. One topic per two days = 24 days, plus 4 rest days, plus 3 days of general revision.

- Monday and Tuesday: *Electric Counterpoint*
- Wednesday and Thursday: 'Something's Coming'
- Etc.

Ideally, draw up detailed plans of each day. People tend to revise most effectively in short concentrated bursts of about 20 minutes to half an hour, so structure your revision around sessions of this length, giving yourself plenty of breaks in which to switch off. Start each revision session by reminding and testing yourself of what you learnt in the previous session. As you are revising for a listening exam, you should also make sure that you include plenty of time to **listen** to the set works in your revision plan: it is important that you get to know the **sound** of the music, rather than just learning facts about it. Don't be too ambitious about what you can achieve in a day as you will soon get behind: 6–8 hours of revision (including short breaks) is a realistic maximum.

EXAMPLE 3

Wednesday:

9.00–9.20	Go through the 'test yourself' questions on Tuesday's topics, writing out the answers
9.20–9.30	Break
9.30–9.50	*Skye Waulking Song:* revise background to folk music and waulking
9.50–10.00	Break
10.00–10.30	*SWS*: revise instrumentation, texture and structure
10.30–10.45	Break
10.45–11.05	*SWS*: revise melody, harmony and rhythm and metre
11.05–11.15	Break
11.15–11.45	*SWS*: test yourself questions; listen to the recording, without any books, and write down key musical features
11.45–12.00	Break

Once you have a plan, do your best to stick to it, otherwise you will need to spend more time devising another plan.

2. TACKLE THE WORKS YOU ARE LEAST CONFIDENT ABOUT FIRST

If you leave the most unfamiliar works to last, you will become more anxious about them and may not be able to spend enough time on them. By approaching them first, you will give yourself more time to get to grips with them when you are least pressurised, and feel more confident about the exam.

3. FOCUS ON REMEMBERING THESE KEY FACTS ABOUT EACH WORK

1. When it was written
2. Where it was written
3. Where it would be performed
4. Its musical style/tradition
5. Any unusual instruments that are playing in it

6. Its structure
7. **Two** facts about each of:
   - Rhythm and metre
   - Melody
   - Harmony and tonality
   - Texture and instrumentation/use of technology
8. The meaning of any technical terms and unusual symbols printed in the score.

You might find it helpful to highlight these points in this revision guide to help focus your revision.

4. LISTEN TO THE SET WORKS AS MUCH AS POSSIBLE

If you are able to, buy or borrow the CD of set works, or download the tracks from the internet onto your computer or music player (remember to download the correct versions, as some set works have been recorded by a number of different performing forces). You can then **listen to them regularly** and practise spotting the features of harmony, melody, rhythm and so on that you need to learn. Ask your teacher for help if you can't get hold of the tracks.

5. USE PRACTICE PAPERS

Ask your teacher if they can give you some **practice papers**. When completing these, try to do so in exam conditions. If they have time, ask your teacher if they can mark them and help you with any questions you were unsure about. Then have another go at these questions to give you confidence if anything similar appears in your exam. If your teacher doesn't have time, they may be able to give you a mark scheme for you to use yourself.

The *Edexcel GCSE Music Listening Tests* from Rhinegold Education includes three complete practice papers, as well as general advice to help you develop your listening skills.

6. PRACTISE WRITING EXTENDED ANSWERS

The idea of writing an extended answer in an exam may seem daunting, but if you practise writing them beforehand you will be much more confident. Aim to write an extended answer on each set work as part of your revision: there are practice questions in the Rhinegold Education Edexcel *GCSE Music Study Guide* or *GCSE Music Listening Tests*.

The main type of question you will be asked in the exam will go something like: 'Comment on how the following musical elements are used in this piece: metre and rhythm; melody; harmony and tonality; instruments and voices'. Valid points covering all the musical elements are given for each set work in this revision guide, so you can plan extended answers around these.

Generally speaking, when answers like this are being marked, you will be credited for each relevant **musical** feature you describe. So try to make points such as:

- There is frequent use of cross rhythms
- The texture is homophonic throughout the work.

Avoid vague descriptions, such as 'the melody here is very beautiful' or 'the rhythm is quite interesting'.

Also avoid giving any information that is not asked for in the question, for example biographical information about the composer's life (such as 'Mozart was born in 1756 and died in 1791'), or opinions (such as 'I like this piece the least of the set works').

7. CARRY OUT YOUR OWN RESEARCH

You are much more likely to remember things that you have **found out for yourself**. Try looking through books in your school or local library, or use websites such as Wikipedia, Spotify, the BBC website, YouTube and Google. It's much easier to remember an artist's name or identify an instrument if you've seen a photo or video of them.

8. KEEP A NOTEBOOK

Every time you come across a word you don't recognise or have forgotten, look it up in the glossary and **write out the word and its meaning** in the notebook. Note an **example** of where it appears in one of the set works. Read through and test yourself regularly on these words until you have learned them by heart.

9. REVISE IN A QUIET, DISTRACTION-FREE PLACE

Unless you are using them for revision, **avoid distractions** such as the internet, background music and your mobile. Consider revising in your local library, where it is much harder to get distracted.

10. USE YOUR OWN INSTRUMENTAL KNOWLEDGE

Try to **make connections between what you are learning and music you have played** or know well. For instance, have you played or sung any Baroque music, and what similarities does it have with the set work by Handel? Which songs do you know that most remind you of Moby or Buckley? Have you ever heard any music that is as dissonant as Schoenberg? Asking yourself questions like these will help you to gain a deeper understanding of the set works and help to reinforce the facts you already know.

Area of Study 1: western classical music 1600–1899

Baroque music and Handel

The Baroque period of music lasted from around **1600** to **1750**. The word 'Baroque' was used to describe things that were ornate and extravagant, and Baroque music is often very **decorative**, with ornamented melody lines and complex counterpoint. The Baroque period was the first in which composers thought as much in terms of harmony (chords) as polyphony (individual lines), and this way of thinking formed the basis of music for the next 300 years.

KEY FEATURES

1. **Simple**, mainly **diatonic** harmonies
2. Movements that usually keep to the **same mood** throughout
3. **Terraced dynamics** – changes in volume are **sudden** rather than gradual
4. **Ornamentation** – melodies are often highly decorated
5. Complex **contrapuntal** writing in some pieces
6. Orchestras made up largely of **string** instruments
7. The use of a **continuo** – a group of instruments that provides a bass line and harmonic accompaniment. Usually consists of a **keyboard** instrument (harpsichord or organ), with one or more **bass** instruments (such as cello or double bass).

Four important composers in the Baroque period were **Bach**, **Handel**, **Purcell** and **Vivaldi**.

Handel was born in the same year as Bach, in 1685. He grew up in Germany, spent time in Italy and later settled in London. An excerpt from his most famous piece, *Messiah*, is the first set work.

Handel: 'And the Glory of the Lord' from *Messiah*

'And the Glory of the Lord' comes from the oratorio *Messiah*. An **oratorio** is a large-scale composition for solo singers, choir and orchestra. It is usually based on a Biblical story – the words of *Messiah* are selected from the Bible and refer to important Christian beliefs about the life of Jesus.

Messiah was composed in **1741** while Handel was living in London. It was originally performed in **concert halls** and **theatres** (although today you might also hear it performed in a church). The first performance was given by a **small choir and orchestra**; now it is often performed by much larger forces.

'And the Glory of the Lord' is the **first chorus** in *Messiah*.

PERFORMING FORCES

- The choir is made up of **sopranos**, **altos**, **tenors** and **basses**
- They are accompanied by **strings** and **continuo** (for **cello** and **harpsichord** or **organ**)
- The orchestra often **doubles** the vocal lines.

STRUCTURE

- The work starts with an **orchestral introduction**, called a **ritornello**. Shortened versions of this music return later in the work in two different places.
- There is no set form to the movement. It is based on **different combinations** of the **four motifs** below.

MELODY

The movement is based on **four different motifs**:

First sung by the **altos**, starting in bar 11, it clearly outlines the key of **A major**.

2.

shall   be   re - veal - - - ed,

First sung by the **tenors**, starting in bar 17. This motif uses a **descending sequence** and a **melisma** on the word 'revealed'. (The little '8' under the treble clef in this example means that the music sounds an octave lower than it is written.)

3.

and   all   flesh___   shall   see___   it   to - ge - ther,

First sung by the **altos**, starting in bar 43. The short descending figure from A to E is repeated twice.

4.

for   the   mouth   of   the Lord   hath   spo - ken   it.

First sung by the **tenors and basses**, starting in bar 51. As most of it is on the same pitch (A), and it uses longer notes, it sounds rather **solemn**.

These four motifs are heard in different parts and combined in different ways throughout the movement.

RHYTHM, METRE AND TEMPO

- The piece is in the dance-like metre of $\frac{3}{4}$ – three crotchet beats per bar.
- It maintains a **fast** tempo (**Allegro**) almost until the end, when there is a bar of total silence (known as a **general pause**), and then three bars in a slower tempo (marked **Adagio**) to create a drawn-out ending.
- There are a number of **hemiolas** in the piece, such as at bars 9–10 (where the music feels as if it is in $\frac{2}{4}$ rather than $\frac{3}{4}$).

TONALITY AND HARMONY

- The piece is in **A major**. It modulates to two related keys: the dominant (**E major**) and the supertonic (**B major**). The work ends with a **plagal cadence** in A major.
- The harmony is **diatonic**.

TEXTURE

- Most of the piece alternates between **homophonic** and **contrapuntal** passages. For example, the first passage sung by the whole choir is **homophonic** (bars 14–17). This is then followed by a **contrapuntal** section that introduces the phrase 'shall be revealed' (bars 17–33).
- There is a very short **monophonic** passage in bars 108–9.
- Handel uses **imitation**. For example, in bar 17 the tenors sing 'shall be revealed' and this is then **imitated** (overlapped by a copy of the same melody, here at a different pitch) by the basses and sopranos.
- The number of parts **varies** – sometimes it is just one (such as altos in bars 43–46), and at other times it is two or three parts (in different combinations) or all four vocal parts together.

WORD SETTING

- There is a mixture of **syllabic** and **melismatic** word setting. For example, motif 4 above ('For the mouth of the Lord hath spoken it') is syllabic. Whereas the word 'revealed' in motif 2 is melismatic.
- The different phrases of text are **repeated many times**, helping to make the words as clear as possible.

Test yourself on 'And the glory of the Lord'

1. In which decade was this work composed?

    (a) 1680s   (b) 1710s   (c) 1740s   (d) 1770s

2. In which country did Handel compose this work?

3. From what type of work is the movement 'And the glory of the Lord' taken?

4. At the end of the opening instrumental section, a rhythmic device is used in which a $\frac{2}{4}$ metre is suggested, although the movement is in $\frac{3}{4}$. What is the name for this device?

5. What does the term 'continuo' mean?

6. The tenor part is written using the clef 𝄞. Which of the following does this clef indicate?

    (a) the music sounds an octave higher than written

    (b) the music sounds at the same pitch as written

    (c) the music sounds an octave lower than written

    (d) the singers of this line should sing their part falsetto

7. What type of cadence ends the movement?

8. What does the term 'imitation' mean?

9. When the tenors first sing 'shall be revealed', a melodic sequence is used. Describe what is meant by 'melodic sequence'.

10. In the same passage the tenors also use a melisma on the word 'revealed'. What does 'melisma' mean?

11. Towards the end of the piece, there is a short section where the soprano and violins perform a single melodic line unaccompanied. What is the name for this type of texture?

12. Name **three** key features of Baroque music.

Classical music and Mozart

The Classical period in music lasted from about **1750** to **1825**. It was an age in which composers reacted against some of the more complex aspects of the Baroque style. Instead, there was a preference for simple **homophonic** textures, melodies formed from **balanced phrases** and **clear cadences** to define the keys and structure of the music.

KEY FEATURES

1. **Balanced** and **clear-cut** phrases that form **questions and answers**
2. More **contrasts** within a movement compared to the Baroque period (such as contrasts in texture or instrumentation)
3. Changes in **dynamic** are not always as sudden as in the Baroque period, as composers now use **crescendos** and **diminuendos**
4. Textures are often **simpler** than in the Baroque period, and often **homophonic**
5. The harpsichord is replaced with the **piano**
6. Orchestras now usually include a range of **wind instruments** – although the melody is usually heard in the **strings**.

Important composers in the Classical period were **Mozart**, **Haydn** and **Beethoven**.

Mozart was a child prodigy and toured Europe, giving performances to royalty, at the age of seven. He lived in Salzburg, Paris and Vienna, and even though he died when he was only 35, he left over 600 compositions. He is the composer of the next set work.

Mozart: Symphony No. 40 in G minor (first movement)

Symphony No. 40 was one of Mozart's last symphonies, written in **1788**. It was intended to be performed in a **large room of a stately home** or a **small concert hall**. The symphony has **four** movements; we are studying the **first** one.

PERFORMANCE MARKINGS

You will find the following markings in the score:

div. (viola part)	The players **divide** into two groups
1	A **single** person plays this part
a 2	**Both** players play this part
sf	Accent
tr	Trill

STRUCTURE AND TONALITY

This movement is in **sonata form**, in the key of **G minor**.

Section	Sub-section	Description	Key
Exposition	First subject	A melody that is characterised by a **falling motif** to the repeated rhythm ♫ ♩ Played by **strings** at first	G minor
	Second subject	A melody with **descending chromatic patterns**, shared between **strings** and **woodwind**	B♭ major (relative major)
Development		Based on the **first subject**, which is **developed** and **fragmented**	Moves through various keys (starts in F♯ minor)
Recapitulation	First subject	The first subject is repeated with **some variation**	G minor
	Second subject	The second subject is repeated with **some variation**	G minor
	Coda	Repeated **perfect cadences** in **G minor** finish the piece	G minor

MELODY

- Most of the melodies are made up of **balanced**, **four-** or **eight-bar** phrases that sound like **questions and answers**. For example, the **second subject** starts with a four-bar phrase that ends with an imperfect cadence – it sounds like a question. This is followed by a four-bar phrase that ends with a perfect cadence, and makes up the answer.
- Many phrases are **scalic** (based on scales).
- See the table above for a description of the first and second subjects.

HARMONY

The harmony is **diatonic** and **functional**, based around standard major and minor triads. We can also find examples of:

- **Chromatic chords**, such as the diminished 7th and augmented 6th
- A **circle of 5ths progression** (in the second subject)
- **Pedal notes**, which the cellos have just before the second subject starts.

RHYTHM, METRE AND TEMPO

- The **metre** is $\frac{4}{4}$ throughout.
- The **tempo** is 'Molto Allegro' – **very fast**.
- **Short rhythmic ideas** are **repeated** to create unity. For example, the **first subject** begins with an **anacrusis** of **two quavers**, which is followed by a **crotchet**. This rhythm (♫ ♩) **recurs throughout the first subject**.
- Rhythms are **fairly simple**, although there are some **dotted rhythms** and **syncopation** to help create momentum and add interest.

TEXTURE

The texture is mostly **homophonic**. We can also find examples of:

- **Counterpoint** and **imitation** in the **development**
- **Octave doublings**, which are frequently used
- **Dialogue** between the **woodwind** and **strings** at the start of the **second subject**.

DYNAMICS

1. In the **exposition**:
   - Apart from a short passage in the middle, the **first subject** is **quiet**
   - The **transition** is **loud**
   - The **second subject** begins **quietly** and **gets louder** towards the end.
2. The **development** has a **loud section** in the middle, but **starts and ends quietly**.
3. The **recapitulation** has similar dynamics to the exposition.

Most dynamic contrasts occur **suddenly** – there are only a few crescendos and no diminuendos.

USE OF INSTRUMENTS

Mozart uses a **chamber orchestra** made up of **strings**, **woodwind** and **horns**.

- The **strings** are busy almost all of the time. They play a variety of material, such as the melody, quick running scales, sustained notes and forceful chords.
- The **woodwind** don't play quite so much, and tend to have **more sustained notes**, and **fewer quick runs** than the strings. They **share** the **start of the second subject** with the strings.
- The two **horns** are in **different keys** (one in G and the other in B♭), which **maximises the number of notes** they can play between them. The horns mostly play **held or repeated notes** to **sustain harmonies**.

Test yourself on Symphony No. 40

1. In which decade was this work written?

    (a) 1720s   (b) 1750s   (c) 1780s   (d) 1810s

2. In what type of place would it have been originally performed?

3. Do most of the dynamics in the first movement change suddenly or gradually?

4. Name **two** harmonic features that can be found in this movement.

5. Why did Mozart use horns in two different keys?

6. Write out the short rhythm that characterises the first subject.
   (Clue: it lasts for 2 beats.)

7. Name the form of this movement. What are the three main sections
   of this form?

8. This work was composed in the Classical period. Which one of the following is a
   common type of phrase structure used in this period?

    (a) call and response

    (b) question and answer

    (c) subject and countersubject

    (d) verse and chorus

9. To which key does the music modulate for the first appearance of the second subject,
   and what is its relationship with the tonic key of the work (G minor)?

10. Which **two** instrumental families share the start of the second subject?

    (a) horns   (b) strings   (c) woodwind

11. What does the performance marking 'div.' mean?

12. Name another composer from the Classical period.

AREA OF STUDY 1: WESTERN CLASSICAL MUSIC 1600–1899

Romantic music and Chopin

The Romantic period lasted from around **1825** to **1900**. In contrast to the Classical period, which focused on form and structure, Romantic music often centred on **conveying emotions**, **telling stories** and **painting musical pictures**. Composers started to free themselves from convention to create their own more personal styles, and **virtuoso** performers, such as Liszt and Paganini, became celebrities. Orchestras continued to expand, and public concerts and amateur music-making became increasingly popular.

KEY FEATURES

1. Music is more **expressive** and **emotional** than in earlier periods
2. **Rich** and **chromatic** harmonies are used, with a greater use of **dissonance**, and **modulations** to more **remote** keys
3. **Technical advances** in instruments are exploited, which in part leads to **larger orchestras** and the rise of the **virtuoso**
4. Structures and forms become **longer**
5. Pieces are often given **descriptive** titles, and **programme music** becomes more common.

Important composers in the Romantic period include **Liszt**, **Mendelssohn**, **Schumann** and **Chopin**.

Chopin was a Polish composer who wrote nearly all of his music for solo piano. He spent most of his career in Paris, where he taught, composed and gave concerts to small, select gatherings of people, events that were known as 'salons'. He is the composer of the next set work.

Chopin: Prelude No. 15 in D♭

This piece is nicknamed the '**Raindrop**' prelude, possibly because of the **repeated quavers** that can be heard throughout (which sound like raindrops falling steadily).

It comes from a collection of preludes by Chopin known as **Op. 28** (work number 28), composed in **1839**. There are **24 preludes** in total: one in each of the 12 major and 12 minor keys.

You are most likely to hear this piece performed in a **small** space, such as in the home, a recital room or a small concert hall.

STRUCTURE

Ternary form (ABA):

A	D♭ major	A lyrical melody accompanied by quavers in the bass. This section also has its own ABA structure.
B	C♯ minor	In contrast to the first section, the melody, which is new, is now in the bass and the quavers are heard above it. The music has moved from major to minor and builds up to a couple of **ff** climaxes.
A	D♭ major	A return to the opening melody. This repeat of Section A is shorter and finishes with a brief coda.

PERFORMANCE MARKINGS

You will find the following markings in the score:

Phrase marks (‿)	Indicates phrases that should be played legato
Ped.	Press down the sustaining pedal
*	Release the sustaining pedal
<	Crescendo (cresc.) – gradually get louder
>	Diminuendo (dim.) – gradually get quieter
Sotto voce	Play quietly (like a musical whisper)
Smorzando	Dying away
Slentando / ritenuto	Slow down
✕	Double sharp – raise the note by 2 semitones (in bar 42, F✕ is the same as G♮)

RHYTHM, METRE AND TEMPO

- The time signature **C** is the same as $\frac{4}{4}$ time – four crotchet beats per bar.
- One unusual rhythmic feature is the **septuplet** in bars 4 and 23: seven notes of equal length are played in a single crotchet beat.
- In bar 79 there is a **dectuplet**: ten notes of equal length fit into a single beat.
- 'Sostenuto' is written at the start of the score. This means 'sustained' – the piece should be played in a **legato, unhurried manner**.
- **Rubato** is used in the recorded performance. The pianist plays some notes longer than written and others shorter than written, creating a flexible tempo for expressive effect.
- **Repeated quavers** are a unifying rhythmic feature throughout the piece.
- The melody begins with a **dotted rhythm**. This is repeated a number of times in **Section A**, helping to give it a lighter feel than the melody of Section B.

MELODY

- The prelude begins with a **lyrical** melody in the **right hand**. It is decorated with **ornaments**, such as an **acciaccatura** (in bar 4) and a **turn** (in bar 11). The melody features **dotted rhythms** and some **chromaticism**.
- In Section B the melody moves to the **bass**. It has a **narrower range** and is mostly made up of **longer notes** (crotchets and minims).
- The prelude is mostly made up of **four-** and **eight-bar** phrases.

TONALITY AND HARMONY

- The prelude is in **D♭ major**. It uses mainly **diatonic harmony** with **occasional chromaticism**.
- The piece modulates from the **tonic major** (D♭ major) in Section A to the **enharmonic tonic minor** (C♯ minor) in Section B. It returns to D♭ major for the repeat of Section A.
- Sections A and B both end with **imperfect cadences**. The prelude ends with a **perfect cadence**.
- There is a **dominant pedal** that can be heard throughout most of the piece (the repeated A♭s in Section A and the repeated G♯s in Section B).

TEXTURE

Apart from two bars towards the end of the piece, the texture is **homophonic**.

- **Section A**: melody in the right hand, supported by **broken chords** in the left hand.
- **Section B**: melody passes into the left hand, with repeated quavers (the **dominant pedal**) in the right hand. The pedal is **inverted** (in the top part rather than the bass) for much of this section, and it is **doubled in octaves** each time the music builds to a climax. The texture of this section is more **chordal** than Section A.
- **Section A**: back to the opening texture. There is a short **monophonic** passage in the coda.

DYNAMICS

- Chopin uses a lot of **crescendos** and **diminuendos**
- There is a **wide range** of dynamics (from *pp* to *ff*) but **no sudden contrasts**
- Section A is **quieter** than Section B, which climaxes to *ff* **twice**.

USE OF THE PIANO

- Most of the prelude uses the **middle** and **lower** ranges of the piano.
- Unlike some of Chopin's other works, the piano writing is **not virtuoso** in character. Instead, Chopin concentrates on the piano's ability to produce a **legato**, **singing** tone.
- Chopin exploits the piano's **wide dynamic range**, with much use of **crescendos** and **diminuendos**.
- The **sustaining pedal** is used for resonance to help create legato melodies.

Test yourself on Prelude No. 15

1. This piece comes from a collection of 24 preludes (Op. 28) by Chopin. What is special about the keys used for the 24 preludes?

2. At what type of occasion did Chopin normally perform his music when he lived in Paris?

3. Why is this work often referred to as the 'Raindrop' prelude?

4. Name the term for the 'flexible tempo' that might be used when performing this work.

5. What do the performance markings 'smorzando' and 'slentando' mean?

6. This work makes frequent use of pedal notes. What is a pedal note?

7. What is the form of this work?

8. What do the symbols 'Ped.' and * mean?

9. What is the key of the central section of the work? What is the relationship of this key to the tonic, D♭ major?

10. What type of texture does most of this work use?

11. What is the difference between a septuplet and a dectuplet?

12. Describe **three** differences between music in the Classical and Romantic periods.

Area of Study 2: music in the 20th century

Expressionism and Schoenberg

Expressionism was an early 20th century movement in the arts, in which the aim was to **express feelings** as **intensely as possible**. Rather than trying to create life-like and realistic paintings, Expressionist artists would use distortion and unnatural colours to portray their emotions. Expressionist art is often dark and moody, but it can also communicate feelings of happiness and joy.

Schoenberg was an important figure in the Expressionist movement. He was an Austrian composer who founded the **Second Viennese School** – a group of composers (including **Berg** and **Webern**, who were taught by Schoenberg in Vienna) who wrote Expressionist music.

Schoenberg was a pioneer of **atonal** music – music that is not in any key. The next set work, 'Peripetie', is one of his early atonal works.

Schoenberg: 'Peripetie' from *Five Orchestral Pieces*

The *Five Orchestral Pieces,* composed in **1909**, were considered to be quite shocking at the time. It was difficult for Schoenberg to find anyone to perform them, partly because of their **experimental nature** and partly because they required such a **large orchestra**. The first performance was given in 1912 at the Proms in London.

'Peripetie' is the **fourth** of Schoenberg's *Five Orchestral Pieces*. The title means '**A sudden reversal**', which perhaps refers to the fact that ideas from the start of the movement return in **reverse order** towards the end. The version we are studying here comes from a new edition of the work that Schoenberg wrote in 1922.

INSTRUMENTATION

- The work requires a **large orchestra** of at least 90 players (made up of strings, woodwind, a large brass section and percussion)
- The instrumentation changes **rapidly** throughout, creating many **contrasts in timbre**
- Performers are frequently required to play at the **extremes of their range** – either very high or very low

- **Unusual effects** are used – for example, the cymbals are played with both a mallet and a cello bow, and at one point the double basses play a tremolo very close to the bridge that supports their strings.

These instruments in the orchestra might be unfamiliar to you:

- **Piccolo** – a small flute (sounds an octave higher than written in the score)
- **Cor anglais** – a lower version of the oboe
- **Bass clarinet** – a large clarinet (sounds an octave lower than a standard clarinet)
- **Contrabassoon** – a large bassoon (sounds an octave lower than written in the score)
- **Tam-tam** – a large gong.

PERFORMANCE MARKINGS

You will find the following markings in the score:

H⌐ ⌐	Stands for **Haupstimme**, which means **the most important part**
N⌐ ⌐	Stands for **Nebenstimme**, which means **the second most important part**
a 2 or a 3	**All two** or **all three** bassoons (for example) should play the same notes
divisi	The players on this line **divide** into groups
pizz	Short for pizzicato – **pluck** the strings
arco	**Bow** the strings
bell up	The brass player points the **bell** (end) of their instrument upwards, to produce a loud, strident sound
1 solo	A **single** person plays this line
tutti	**Everyone** joins in again
+	**Hand-stopped** – the horn player inserts their hand further than usual into the bell
≣	**Tremolo** – the note is rapidly repeated

MELODY

- 'Peripetie' is made up of many **short**, **fragmented motifs** that are combined in different ways. In the first 18 bars alone, seven different motifs are quickly introduced.
- Melodies are **disjunct** (with many large leaps) and so often sound very **angular** – Schoenberg uses **octave displacement**, unexpectedly moving individual notes of the main melody into a different octave.
- Although motifs aren't really developed or drawn-out to form longer melodies (as in the Romantic period), they are varied through the use of techniques such as **inversion** (a melody is turned upside down) and rhythmic **augmentation** (the notes become twice as long).

RHYTHM, METRE AND TEMPO

- The **metre** changes between $\frac{3}{4}$, $\frac{2}{4}$ and $\frac{4}{4}$.
- The tempo is Sehr rasch – **very quick**.
- Rhythms are **complex** and **varied**, and **change quickly**. In parts of the work, Schoenberg **layers** a number of different rhythmic patterns on top of each other to create a complex contrapuntal texture.

TONALITY AND HARMONY

- The piece is **atonal**. It uses a lot of **dissonant** harmony.
- Chords and melodies are often built from **hexachords** (groups of six notes).

TEXTURE AND DYNAMICS

- The texture is largely **contrapuntal**, with occasional monophonic and homophonic moments
- **Complex** textures are built up through the use of techniques such as **imitation** and **inversion**. For example, the final climax of the piece is created from three different **canons** that are all heard at the same time.
- There are frequent **sudden changes** of dynamics, leading to **extreme contrasts** between *ppp* and *fff*.

STRUCTURE

- This piece is in **free rondo** form, with **five** sections (ABACA). It is called **free** rondo because it is very different to the traditional type of rondo heard in the Classical period, when different sections were clearly contrasted.

Test yourself on 'Peripetie'

1. In which decade was this work composed?

    (a) 1880s   (b) 1900s   (c) 1930s   (d) 1950s

2. With which school of composers is Schoenberg commonly associated?

3. Give **two** possible reasons why this work is not as frequently performed as Mozart's Symphony No. 40.

4. 'Peripetie' is atonal. What does this term mean?

5. What does the symbol $\mathsf{\Pi\,\daleth}$ indicate?

6. What is a contrabassoon?

7. 'Peripetie' uses disjunct melodies. What does this mean?

8. Many of the ideas in this work are based on hexachords. How many notes does a hexachord contain?

9. Stringed instruments are sometimes asked to play 'tremolo'. What does this mean?

10. 'Peripetie' is characterised by sudden contrasts of mood. Describe **three** ways in which this is achieved. (Clue: think about the melodies, use of orchestration, dynamics, and different registers.)

11. Name **two** percussion instruments that play in 'Peripetie'.

12. Which **one** of the following statements is true?

    (a) 'Peripetie' is a serial work

    (b) 'Peripetie' is in sonata form

    (c) 'Peripetie' uses canons

    (d) 'Peripetie' is influenced by Indian rags

Musicals and Bernstein

A **musical** is like a **play** where most of the words are **sung** rather than spoken. It is similar to **opera**, except that the music is usually in a **popular style**, designed to be sung by **actors** instead of professional singers.

Early musicals developed in the **1920s**. They were formed mainly from **songs** linked by **acted scenes** to make a story. Over time, the acted and sung elements became more successfully integrated and the stories more weighty. The music became more sophisticated, too, with some composers drawing on the rhythms and harmonies of **20th century classical music** and **jazz**.

The American composer **Leonard Bernstein** wrote one of the most famous musicals, *West Side Story,* from which the next set work is taken. Aside from composing works in many different genres, Bernstein was also a skilled pianist, conductor and broadcaster. He was influenced by jazz and the music of 20th century composers such as Stravinsky.

Bernstein: 'Something's Coming' from *West Side Story*

West Side Story was composed in **1957**. The musical is based on Shakespeare's famous play *Romeo and Juliet*. Set in **New York**, it features two rival teenage gangs, the **Jets** (American) and the **Sharks** (Puerto Rican). **Tony**, the male lead character (and a Jet) falls in love with **Maria** (from the Sharks). As in *Romeo and Juliet*, their love is ultimately doomed.

The song 'Something's Coming' is **Tony's first solo**, and establishes his optimistic character.

INSTRUMENTATION

- 'Something's Coming' is a song for **solo tenor** accompanied by a band made up of **woodwind**, **brass**, **percussion** and **strings**.
- To make sure the band doesn't overpower the solo singer, the accompaniment uses:
  - **Quiet dynamics**
  - **Soft timbres**, such as muted trumpets and pizzicato strings
  - A **homophonic texture**.
- Listen out for the two techniques used in the accompaniment to illustrate the words 'The air is humming': the strings use **harmonics** (very high notes) and play **tremolo** (very quick notes).

STRUCTURE AND MELODY

The melody is almost entirely **syllabic**. It is based on the alternation of **three main themes**:

1. The **quiet, syncopated opening theme**
2. The **loud, strident theme** in $\frac{2}{4}$, first heard at bar 21
3. The **lyrical, slow-moving theme**, first heard at bar 73.

These three ideas are **alternated** a number of times. The repetitions are **not exact**, and Bernstein **varies** the themes by changing such things as the **words** or **metre**.

RHYTHM, METRE AND TEMPO

- The **metre** changes between $\frac{3}{4}$ and $\frac{2}{4}$.
- These **changes of metre**, the **fast tempo** and the frequent **syncopation** help to maintain a feeling of **excitement** and **anticipation**.
- The **accompaniment** is largely made up of an **on-beat bass part** with **off-beat chords**. At the start of the piece, these two parts create **cross rhythms**.

HARMONY AND TONALITY

- 'Something's Coming' is in **D major**. There are **two contrasting sections** in **C major**.
- There is **frequent use** of the **sharpened fourth** and **flattened seventh** in both keys (G♯ and C♮ in the D major sections, and F♯ and B♭ in the C major sections). The sharpened fourth creates the interval of a **tritone** with the key note, an interval that acts as a unifying feature throughout *West Side Story*.
- The tenor's **last note** is a **flattened seventh** (C♮ against D major harmonies). This is unusual as the note is **unresolved** and the music just fades out beneath it. It creates a feeling of **incompletion** and fits well with Tony's sense of **expectation**.
- The harmony is **tonal** and **jazz-influenced**, with **frequent 7th chords** and other **added note chords**.

TEXTURE

The texture of the song is **homophonic**. There are **three** main ideas in the accompaniment:

1. The **repeated riff** that opens the song
2. The **short**, mainly **syncopated chords** heard in bars 21–26
3. A **fast, um-cha accompaniment** first heard at bar 32 for the long note on 'me'.

Test yourself on 'Something's Coming'

1. On which Shakespeare play is *West Side Story* based?

2. In which year was *West Side Story* first performed?

    (a) 1935   (b) 1946   (c) 1957   (d) 1968

3. Name the **two** different metres used in this song.

4. What unusual interval recurs throughout this song and the rest of *West Side Story*?

5. Is the melody largely melismatic or syllabic?

6. What musical term best describes the repeated accompaniment pattern that opens the song?

7. What **two** instrumental techniques does Bernstein use to illustrate the words 'The air is humming'?

8. What is the texture of this song?

    (a) homophonic   (b) monophonic   (c) polyphonic

9. What musical term is used to describe two conflicting rhythms heard at the same time?

10. How is the second theme (first heard at bar 21) different to the opening vocal melody?

11. *West Side Story* was originally written to be performed without amplifying the voices. In 'Something's Coming', how does Bernstein ensure the instruments do not drown out the voice?

12. How does Bernstein create a sense of expectation at the end of the song?

Minimalism and Steve Reich

Minimalism is a style of music that developed in the late 1960s as a reaction against the complexity of modernist music. Features of minimalism include:

1. The **repetition of simple ideas** with **small changes introduced gradually** over time
2. Melodies slowly built up through the process of **note addition**
3. **Layered textures**
4. **Diatonic harmony**
5. **Slow harmonic rhythm**
6. **Little variety in instrumentation**.

All of these features can be found in the next set work by **Steve Reich**. Reich is an American composer who is still alive today. His work shows such diverse influences as African drumming, Hebrew chant and gamelan music. Some of his early pieces were greeted with much controversy when they were first performed.

Other minimalist composers include **Philip Glass** and **John Adams**.

Reich: Electric Counterpoint (third movement)

Electric Counterpoint was written for the famous jazz guitarist **Pat Metheny**, who gave the first performance of the work in **1987**. It is in **three** movements, which follow a typical fast–slow–fast pattern. We are studying the **third** movement.

INSTRUMENTATION

- This movement is for **live guitar**, accompanied by parts for **seven guitars** and **two bass guitars** that have been **pre-recorded** (although the work can be played entirely by live guitarists if preferred).
- The live guitar part is **amplified** to blend in well with the backing tape.

STRUCTURE

The movement builds up in **three layers**:

1. A **syncopated quaver motif** is introduced in the **live guitar** and **top four guitar** parts, **one part at a time**
2. A new **syncopated quaver motif** is next introduced in the **bass guitars**
3. A more **sustained motif**, built around **three chords**, begins in the **live guitar** part and is then **transferred to other parts**.

After all three layers have been built up, layers 2 and 3 **fade out** together, leaving layer 1 to continue until it comes to rest on a held chord.

MELODY AND TEXTURE

- The melody is made up of a **one-bar motif** that is **repeated continuously** to form an **ostinato**.
- This motif is introduced by the live guitar and top four guitar parts **at different times**, creating a **canon**.
- In some of the parts, Reich builds up the melody through the process of **note addition**. This means that notes are **gradually added** to a part until **all** the notes in the melody are heard. For example, the live guitar starts with only **three** notes of the motif. After a couple of bars, another **two** notes are added. Then after two more bars, **all** the gaps are filled in and the whole motif is heard.
- At one point the live guitar plays a melody that is made up from selected individual notes from the other guitar parts, creating a **resultant melody**.
- The piece has a **contrapuntal** texture.

RHYTHM, METRE AND TEMPO

- The **main metre** is $\frac{3}{2}$ – three minim beats per bar. Each minim is split into four quavers, which means there are **12 quavers** per bar.
- The tempo is $\downarrow$ = 192, so there are 192 crotchets per minute – a **very fast** speed.
- There is **little rhythmic variety** – most of the piece is made up of **repeating patterns** of **quavers**.
- There is frequent **syncopation**.
- Reich uses an effect called **metrical displacement** – guitars 1–4 play the **same motif** but start in **different parts** of the bar. They sound **out of synch** with each other.
- Towards the end of the piece, some parts go into $\frac{12}{8}$ while others continue in $\frac{3}{2}$. This combination of different time signatures is an example of **polymetre**.

HARMONY AND TONALITY

- The music is largely in the key of **G major**, with some shorter sections towards the end in **E♭ major**. It is entirely **diatonic**.
- Reich uses **hexatonic** scales. For example, the **first motif** is hexatonic – it uses **six notes** of the G major scale.
- Conventional harmonic progressions (such as cadences) **aren't used**. For example, the **final chord** is made up of **only two notes**, **B** and **E**; because there is **no cadence** and it **isn't a complete chord**, we can't be entirely sure that the piece has finished in G major.

DYNAMICS

- The overall dynamic remains fairly **constant** throughout
- Parts gradually **fade out** in a number of places.

Test yourself on *Electric Counterpoint*

1. In which decade was *Electric Counterpoint* composed?

    (a) 1910s   (b) 1950s   (c) 1980s   (d) 1990s

2. Describe **two** ways in which music technology is used in a performance of *Electric Counterpoint*.

3. What is the tempo of *Electric Counterpoint*?

    (a) ♩ = 112   (b) ♩ = 152   (c) ♩ = 192   (d) ♩ = 232

4. The guitar parts use frequent syncopation. What is syncopation?

5. The opening four guitar parts could be described as canonic. What does this mean?

6. Much of the material is based on repeated melodic phrases. What term is used to describe a constantly repeated phrase or rhythm?

7. In this piece the solo guitar picks out notes from the other parts to produce a new melody. What is the name for this type of melody?

8. Some of the melodies used in *Electric Counterpoint* are based on six notes. What is the name for a scale consisting of six notes?

9. Explain what 'note addition' means.

10. Which of the following words best describes the harmony of this piece?

    (a) chromatic   (b) diatonic   (c) modal   (d) whole-tone

11. Name **three** characteristic features of minimalism that can be found in *Electric Counterpoint*.

12. Name **two** other minimalist composers.

Area of Study 3: popular music in context

Jazz and Miles Davis

Jazz is a type of music that originated in the **southern states of America** during the **early 20th century**. Over time, many different styles of jazz have developed which make use of all sorts of line-ups, from a single piano to a swing band. The main element that unites most of these styles is **improvisation**, which refers to music being made up on the spot during a performance.

Miles Davis is one of the best-known **jazz trumpeters**, and has been influential in the development of a number of new jazz styles. One of these is **modal jazz**, which Miles Davis experimented with in the **1950s** as a reaction against the complexity of bebop.

Bebop was a **fast** and **virtuosic** type of jazz, with improvisations based on **complex chord progressions**. In contrast, modal jazz was more **laid-back** and **uncomplicated**, with improvisations based on **modes**.

The next set work, 'All Blues', is an example of Miles Davis' modal jazz.

Miles Davis: All Blues

'All Blues' comes from the album ***Kind of Blue***, released in **1959**. The band on this album is a **sextet** (a group of six players) made up of:

The **frontline**:
1. Miles Davis on **trumpet**
2. Julian 'Cannonball' Adderley on **alto saxophone**
3. John Coltrane on **tenor saxophone**.

The **rhythm section**:
4. Bill Evans on **piano**
5. Paul Chambers on **bass**
6. Jimmy Cobb on **drums**.

The **frontline** consists of the instruments that play the **main melody** and have prominent **solos**. The **rhythm section** provides the **harmonic and rhythmic backing** (although the pianist also has a short solo).

The album was recorded with almost **no rehearsal**, and the musicians had **no score** to play from. Instead, Miles Davis gave them some basic information about the pieces they were about to record:

- The **overall structure**, including who would solo and in which order
- The basic **chord sequence**
- The **main melodic idea**
- Which **mode** or **scale** to improvise on.

STRUCTURE

- 'All Blues' is based on the **12-bar blues progression** – a **chord sequence** that lasts for **12 bars** and **returns throughout the piece**. **One statement** of the chord sequence is called a **chorus**.
- The main melody is called the **head** and is played by **muted trumpet**. It lasts for **12 bars**, and can be heard near the start and at the end of the piece.
- There is a simple **4-bar riff** in **parallel 3rds** that separates each section.

So, the piece can be broken down into **five** sections:

1. **Introduction** – the **opening four bars**, played by the **rhythm section**, is followed by the **riff**
2. **Head 1** – the **head melody**, followed by the **riff**, is played **twice**
3. **Solos** – for **trumpet**, **alto sax**, **tenor sax** and **piano**, each followed by the **riff**
4. **Head 2** – the **head melody**, followed by the **riff**, is played **twice**
5. **Coda** – a solo for **muted trumpet**.

This structure is known as a **head arrangement**.

Intro	Head 1		Solos				Head 2		Coda
Rhythm section	Head melody (trumpet)	Head melody (trumpet)	Trumpet solo	Alto sax solo	Tenor sax solo	Piano solo	Head melody (trumpet)	Head melody (trumpet)	Trumpet solo

(The thin white strips in this table represent the **riff**.)

MELODY

The **head melody** is quite **simple** and characterised by **rising 6ths** (the interval from D to B). This is followed by **four improvised solos**:

1. **Trumpet solo**: lasts for **4 choruses**. Mostly made up of **short, syncopated motifs**.

2. **Alto sax solo**: lasts for **4 choruses**. Uses **quicker notes** and a **wider range**; Adderley's improvisation is more **virtuosic** than Davis'.
3. **Tenor sax solo**: lasts for **4 choruses**. Uses **fast scales** and **quick runs**; also very **virtuosic**.
4. **Piano solo**: lasts for **2 choruses**. This improvisation is **calmer**, with a **simple melody** that leads into a string of **parallel chords**.

HARMONY AND TONALITY

'All Blues' is based on the following **12-bar blues sequence**, which is repeated throughout the piece:

1	2	3	4	5	6	7	8	9	10	11	12
G^7	G^7	G^7	G^7	Gm^7	Gm^7	G^7	G^7	D^7	Eb^7/D^7	F / G	F / G^6

A chord sequence is known by jazz musicians as the **changes**.

We can think of 'All Blues' as being in **G major** but with a **flattened seventh** (a flattened note like this in jazz is called a **blue note**):

This is the same as the **Mixolydian mode**, so we can also describe 'All Blues' as being an example of **modal jazz**.

RHYTHM, METRE AND TEMPO

The score is notated in $^6_4$. The tempo is described as a **jazz waltz** because each $^6_4$ bar sounds like a pair of bars in $^3_4$ time (the metre associated with the waltz).

'All Blues' is performed with **swing quavers**. This means each pair of quavers is played with the first a little longer than the second.

There is frequent **syncopation**.

INSTRUMENTAL TECHNIQUES

The snare drum is played with **wire brushes** at the start – it switches to sticks later on.

The bass plays **pizzicato** throughout.

The trumpet is played with a **Harmon mute** for the head.

The piano plays a **tremolo** at the start of the piece. Once the solos begin, the pianist begins **comping** (accompanying with chords and short melodic ideas).

Test yourself on 'All Blues'

1. In which year was 'All Blues' originally recorded?

    (a) 1937   (b) 1948   (c) 1959   (d) 1966

2. Complete this sentence: ''All Blues' is an example of a jazz form called a .... arrangement'.

3. On what type of chord progression are the choruses in this piece based?

4. Describe the instrumental techniques used by:

    (a) the double bass

    (b) the trumpet when it first plays

    (c) the snare drum at the beginning

5. What is the name for the 4-bar section that separates each chorus?

6. Explain the terms 'frontline' and 'rhythm section'.

7. What is the term for musical ideas that are developed spontaneously, having not previously been written down?

8. Why can 'All Blues' be described as modal jazz?

9. The quavers in 'All Blues' are performed slightly differently to how they are notated in the score. What is the difference?

10. What does the term 'comping' mean, and which instrument does it apply to?

11. With which instrument is Miles Davis associated?

12. Where and when did the blues originate?

Folk rock and Jeff Buckley

Folk music usually refers to the **traditional** music of a country. It is often learned and performed **by ear**; songs are **memorised** and passed down through the generations. In the UK, folk music started to die out in the first half of the 20th century, prompting scholars to write it down and record it. This led to a **folk revival** in the 1950s – popular musicians began to revive traditional songs and to write new ones. Artists such as Bob Dylan and The Byrds combined folk with pop and rock influences, creating the genre of **folk rock** in the 1960s.

Jeff Buckley's music is sometimes described as folk rock, although his songs display many different influences. Buckley was an American singer and guitarist. His father, Tim Buckley, was also a well-known singer who branched out from a folk style. Unfortunately Jeff Buckley only managed to complete one album (*Grace*), before he drowned in a swimming accident at the age of 29.

Buckley: Grace

'Grace' comes from the album *Grace*, released in **1994**. A few of the other tracks from this album are 'Hallelujah', 'Lilac Wine', 'Last Goodbye' and 'Eternal Life' (it might be worth memorising at least one of these, in case you are asked for the name of another track from the album in the exam). 'Grace' is a **rock ballad** – a rock song about love in a slow tempo.

INSTRUMENTATION AND TEXTURE

- Buckley is accompanied by **guitars**, **bass guitar**, **synthesiser**, **strings** and **drum kit**.
- The guitar part in the score is printed in **tab**, which shows the finger positions of each note.
- The guitars use **'drop D tuning'**, which means that the lowest string is tuned down from E to D.
- The **drums and guitars** (playing rhythmic patterns and broken chords) accompany Buckley throughout most of the song. The **synthesiser** and **strings** are less prominent, dropping in and out of the music. They're used to **add effects** or to **vary the texture**.
- The texture **thickens** towards the end of the song, especially in the coda.

USE OF TECHNOLOGY

Various effects are used in this song, including:

- **Modulation** on the synthesiser at the start of the song.
- **Distortion** and **flanging** on the guitars, which help to **intensify** the sound in the **coda**.
- **Overdubbing** on the guitar parts, which creates a **thicker** sound. The **extra vocal parts** in the **bridge** are also produced through overdubbing.
- **EQ** in the **final verse**, which is used to remove the lower frequencies of Buckley's voice.

STRUCTURE

The song has the following **verse-chorus** form:

Intro	Verse 1	Chorus 1	Intro	Verse 2
Instrumental	Voice	Voice ('Wait in the fire')	Instrumental	Voice

Chorus 2	Bridge	Intro	Verse 3	Coda
Voice ('Wait in the fire')	Voice (vocalisation)	Instrumental	Voice	Voice (improvisation)

TONALITY AND HARMONY

- The song is in **E minor**, although the tonality is often **ambiguous** – the introduction focuses on the chord of **D**, for example, so the key of E minor only becomes clear halfway through the first verse.
- The harmony is unusual for a rock song – the standard I–IV–V chord progressions of rock music are avoided. Instead, many of the chords are **chromatic** and move in **parallel motion** (by **semitone steps**, e.g. F–Em–E♭ in the chorus).
- Some of the harmonies are very **dissonant**, particularly in the chorus.

MELODY AND WORD-SETTING

- The vocal part has an **improvised** quality and a very **wide range** of over two octaves.
- Most of the vocal phrases are **falling**, reflecting the **melancholy** mood of the song.
- There is frequent **ornamentation** in the melody line, with **glissandos** (slides) between various notes. These are indicated by a diagonal line:

- Most of the word-setting is **syllabic** (although there are some long **melismas** to emphasise certain words, such as 'love' in verse 1 and 'fire' in the chorus).
- In the bridge there is a passage of **vocalisation** – wordless singing – in which Buckley uses **falsetto**, a technique of singing used for **high** notes.
- The lyrics reflect Buckley's bleak outlook on love. There are many examples of **word painting**; a few of these are:
  - Verse 1: **'cries'** is set to a falling 5th, which sounds like crying
  - Bridge: **'pain'** and **'leave'** are in a very high register and sound fraught
  - Verse 3: **'slow'** is set to a long note
  - Coda: a very thick texture is built up for **'drown** my name'.

RHYTHM, METRE AND TEMPO

- The metre is $\frac{12}{8}$ (a **compound** metre, with **four** dotted-crotchet beats per bar).
- The **bass drum** plays on beats 1 and 3, and the **snare drum** accents the **backbeats** (beats 2 and 4).
- There is frequent **syncopation** in the vocal melody (which is rhythmically very **free**), as well as in the bass line.
- **Cross rhythms** are created through the use of two-against-three rhythms (quavers against dotted quavers).

Test yourself on 'Grace'

1. In which year was 'Grace' released?

   (a) 1973   (b) 1981   (c) 1994   (d) 2004

2. Describe **two** examples of word painting used in this song.

3. In 'Grace', Jeff Buckley sings in a very high register, using a certain vocal technique. What is the name for this technique?

4. What is the form of this song?

5. Which beats of the bar are meant by the term 'backbeat'? Which instrument accentuates these beats in 'Grace'?

6. Apart from drum kit, name **three** instruments that play in this song.

7. Describe **two** ways in which music technology has been used in 'Grace'.

8. Is 'Grace' in a simple or compound metre?

9. Describe how the harmony of 'Grace' differs from that of a typical rock song.

10. What does 'vocalisation' mean?

11. This song is an example of a rock ballad. What is a rock ballad?

12. Other than Jeff Buckley, name a band or artist associated with folk rock.

Club dance music and Moby

Club dance music refers to the electronic music typically played in nightclubs. Its origins are in the 1970s, when club owners started to hire DJs to play records, instead of using live bands for entertainment. In the mid-1970s, disco (the first real type of club dance music) became hugely popular. As technology has become more and more sophisticated and accessible, many sub-genres of club dance music have since developed.

A few **key features** common to most club dance music are:

- A $\frac{4}{4}$ metre and a **steady tempo**
- A prominent use of **electronic** sounds
- A **strong beat**, emphasised by the drums and bass
- **Short phrases** and **repetitive, looped sections**.

Moby (whose real name is Richard Melville Hall) is an American dance musician, born in 1965. He composes music for films as well as dance music. Moby also plays guitar, drums and keyboard, and performs on a regular basis. He started to achieve chart success in the early 1990s. His sixth album, *Play*, is his most successful so far and has sold over nine million copies.

Moby: 'Why Does My Heart Feel So Bad'?

'Why Does My Heart Feel So Bad?' comes from the album ***Play***, which was released in **1999**. Play has 18 tracks (a few of the others are 'Porcelain', 'South Side' and 'Natural Blues'), a number of which contain vocal samples from blues and gospel records. On this album Moby features as a singer, composer, performer, engineer and producer.

SAMPLES AND MELODY

- This song is based on **two samples** taken from a recording made in **1953** of a **gospel choir**, singing an American gospel song called *King Jesus Will Roll All Burdens Away*.
- The first sample (A) is sung by a **male** singer and is used for the **verses**.
- The second sample (B) is sung by a **female** singer and is used in the **chorus**.
- Both samples have been **manipulated** to change the meaning of the words.
- They have a '**vintage**' feel because Moby hasn't cleaned up the surface noise on the recording (the crackles produced when a worn vinyl record is played).
- These samples are **looped** to create the melody, which as a result is simple and repetitive.

STRUCTURE AND TEXTURE

- The song is based on a **verse-chorus** structure
- The samples are **looped** to create the verses and choruses
- After the second verse there is a **breakdown** – one bar's silence.

Intro	Verse				Chorus		Verse			Chorus			Verse
A1	A2	A3	A4	A5	Bx1	By1	A6	A7		Bx2	By2	By3	A8

(A = male sample, B = female sample.)

- The texture is **built up** as individual tracks are introduced one by one:
  - A1: piano only
  - A2: voice enters
  - A3: drums enter, plus a string-synth countermelody
  - A4: bass enters, plus held string-synth chords
  - A5: syncopated piano chords introduced.
- After the breakdown, the texture becomes **thinner** as piano and drums drop out (for Bx2). They re-enter for the next 8 bars (By2), then drop out again until the end.
- **Contrasts** in texture are provided by:
  - Varying instrumentation for each 8-bar section
  - The use of silence
  - Sections with just static chords for the accompaniment.

RHYTHM, TEMPO AND METRE

- The song is in $\frac{4}{4}$ with a **steady** tempo of 98 bpm.
- The drum loop, which enters after 16 bars, is made up of a **breakbeat** (a drum solo) that Moby sampled from a hip-hop track. The **bass drum** plays on beats 1 and 3, while there are strong accents on the **backbeats** (beats 2 and 4) from the **snare drum**. Repeated **semiquavers** are played on the shaker.
- **Syncopation** is used in the piano, vocal and synthesised string parts.
- Rhythms are **varied** between sections to provide contrast. For example, the **piano pattern** changes at the end of the first verse (becoming more syncopated), and **static chords** appear in the second chorus.

USE OF TECHNOLOGY

Moby used the following equipment to produce this track:

- **Synthesisers** – to produce the string, bass and piano sounds
- **Sampler** – used for the vocal samples, as well as the breakbeat rhythm on the drum track
- **Drum machine** – to create the drum track
- **Sequencer** – to trigger the sampler and synthesisers.

Various effects have been applied to the music, for example:

- **Panning** is used to place sounds in the stereo field (e.g. panning on the **piano introduction** creates a sense of movement from left to right and back).
- There are '**electronic ghostings**' on the male vocal sample when it first comes in – these are remnants of the backing singers in the original sample.
- **Reverb** and **delay** are used throughout the track (you can hear the effects of these in the one-bar **breakdown**).
- In the second verse (A6), **echoes** of the voice are created through **delay**. The echoes have been processed with **EQ** to remove the lower frequencies, sounding a bit like listening to a voice on the telephone.

HARMONY AND TONALITY

- The harmony is entirely **diatonic**, made up of **three** simple, repeated chord progressions, each of which lasts for **eight** bars.
- The **first** sample is set to the chord sequence **Am**, **Em**, **G**, **D** (remember this with the mnemonic **Am**azing **Em**ily **G**oes **D**ancing).
- The **second** sample is harmonised in **two** different ways: firstly to **C**, **Am**, **C**, **Am**, and then to the chords **F**, **C**, **F**, **C**.
- We can describe the **verses** as being in the **Dorian mode** on A, and the **choruses** as being in C major.

Test yourself on 'Why Does My Heart Feel So Bad?'

1. When was the track released?

   (a) 1974   (b) 1982   (c) 1990   (d) 1999

2. What is the name of the album from which this song is taken?

3. This track makes extensive use of samples and loops. What is a sample and what is a loop?

4. The vocal samples are taken from gospel music of the 1950s. How can you tell that they are from an old recording?

5. What is a breakbeat?

6. What is the form of this song?

7. Describe **two** ways in which the texture of the song is varied.

8. Name **three** types of digital effect used on this track.

9. Which of the following is a chord sequence used in this song?

   (a) Am, Em, G, D   (b) Am, C, Em, D   (c) Em, G, C, D

10. Which percussion sound plays repeated semiquavers through much of the song?

11. Give **two** examples of timbres that have been produced by synthesisers in this song.

12. List **three** characteristic features of club dance music.

Area of Study 4: world music

Folk music and Capercaillie

Folk music refers to **traditional music** that was originally learnt by ear by each new generation, rather than being notated. Folk music in the UK is centuries old, and has been collected and written down since the 17th century. In the past, folk traditions were in some danger of disappearing, but a **folk revival** in the 1950s sparked new interest in folk music by combining it with pop influences.

The next set work, by the band Capercaillie, is an example of **Celtic fusion**. 'Celtic' means folk music that comes from Wales, Ireland or Scotland. Celtic fusion refers to Celtic folk music that has been combined with elements of pop music.

Capercaillie is a Scottish band that got together at school to play for local folk dances. They started recording albums in 1984 and have created modern arrangements of many traditional songs, including waulking songs.

WAULKING

Waulking is the name given to the process of **pounding tweed cloth** against a wooden board, in order to soften it and make it more airtight. It is work that women undertook by hand in Scotland until around the 1950s. The process used to take many hours, and as the women worked they would sing **waulking songs**.

Waulking songs helped the women to move the cloth **in time** with each other, and also **enlivened** their work. The songs were usually in a **call-and-response** form: the call was sung by a solo singer, and the response by everyone else.

Capercaillie: Skye Waulking Song

'Skye Waulking Song' comes from Capercaillie's album **Nàdurra**, which was released in **2000**. The text for this song is taken from a long **lament** called *John, Son of the King of Ireland*, which takes more than an hour to perform from start to finish.

INSTRUMENTATION AND TEXTURE

A **layered texture** is created through:

- A **rhythmic pattern** on drum kit
- A **bass line** played by bass guitar
- **Chords** on the synthesiser and accordion
- The **main melody** sung by voice
- **Countermelodies** on the other melody instruments (violin, Wurlitzer piano, uilleann pipes and bouzouki).

The three most unusual instruments in this line-up, which you might not have come across before, are:

- The **Wurlitzer piano** – a type of early electric piano
- The **uilleann pipes** – like the bagpipes but with a softer tone
- The **bouzouki** – a type of lute that comes from Greece.

In the score:

- 'N.C.' means 'no chord' – the accompaniment drops out at this point
- The words '**with modulation**' mean that **modulation** (a digital effect) is applied to the **synthesiser chord**, which makes the **pitch fluctuate slightly** (like vibrato). This chord that opens the song is a **cluster chord** – a chord whose notes are all next to each other.

STRUCTURE

The vocal line alternates between **four different phrases** (each lasting for **one bar**) in a **call-and-response** pattern:

- **Phrase 1**: call (in Gaelic, starts on a high D)
- **Refrain 1**: response (vocables, starts on a mid B)
- **Phrase 2**: call (in Gaelic, starts on a low D)
- **Refrain 2**: response (vocables, starts on a high E).

The overall structure is:

1. **Introduction**: an **instrumental section**, after which the **voice enters** with the first line of text
2. **Verse 1**: voice and accompaniment
3. **Verse 2**: voice and accompaniment – this section includes an **instrumental break**
4. **Coda**: **short vocal phrases** echo the end of refrain 1, after which the accompaniment **fades out**.

MELODY

The vocal melody:

- Is **pentatonic** (based on a **five-note scale**)
- Uses a **low register** of the voice – the soloist's part in the score is notated in the **vocal tenor clef**, which means the music sounds an **octave lower** than printed
- Is mainly **syllabic**
- Alternates between one-bar phrases in Gaelic (the **call**) and phrases that use vocables (the **response**). **Gaelic** is a language spoken in some parts of Scotland, and **vocables** are nonsense syllables.

The instrumentalists play **short motifs** and **countermelodies** that are mostly based on the **vocal phrases**. The **main instrumental break**, for example, is based on **refrain 2**.

RHYTHM AND METRE

- The song is notated in $\frac{12}{8}$ (**compound quadruple metre**)
- There is frequent **syncopation** in the vocal line and instrumental countermelodies
- At the start of the song the **hi-hat pattern** creates **cross rhythms**. When the **full band enters**, the hi-hat rhythm **changes** and more clearly **emphasises** $\frac{12}{8}$.

HARMONY

- The song is in **G major**, and is entirely **diatonic**
- The **three main chords** used are **G**, **Em** and **C**
- Because the **dominant chord** (D) is **avoided**, the music has a **modal feel**.

Test yourself on *Skye Waulking Song*

1. Briefly describe what is meant by the term 'waulking'.

2. In a waulking song, who would have traditionally sung the phrases set to Gaelic words, and who would have sung the phrases set to nonsense syllables?

3. This song is an example of 'Celtic fusion'. From which **two** musical styles is Celtic fusion formed?

4. This song features an instrument called a bouzouki. What is this?

5. How many different one-bar phrases is the vocal melody made up of?

6. The rhythm of the hi-hat creates a cross rhythm with the other parts at the start of the song. What is a cross rhythm?

7. The music is in $\frac{12}{8}$. Is this a simple, compound or triple metre?

8. The vocal melody only uses the notes D, E, G, A and B. What type of scale do these notes form?

9. What are the **three** main chords used in this song?

10. In the score, what does the term 'modulation' mean, and which instrument is it applied to?

11. Is the vocal line mainly melismatic or syllabic?

12. Describe how an old folksong would originally have been passed on to other performers.

Indian music and Rag Desh

Rag Desh is an example of **Indian classical music** from north India. Indian classical music has a very long history. It is an **improvised** form of music, although improvisations take place within well-defined structures and conventions. The music is performed by highly skilled musicians who have learned their skills through long years of study with a respected teacher.

KEY FEATURES

Indian classical music is built up of **three** layers:

1. A **melodic line** played on a **solo** instrument
2. A **rhythmic pattern** played on the **drums**
3. A **drone** played on a **stringed** instrument.

MELODY

The melody is based on a **rag**. This is a **pattern of notes**, a little like a **scale**. Different rags are associated with certain times of the day and year.

This set work is based on **rag desh**, which is made up of the following pitches:

Note that the pattern on the way up is **different** on the way down. This rag is associated with the late evening and the monsoon season.

RHYTHM

The rhythmic pattern played by the drums is based on a **tal**. This is a **cycle of beats** that is repeated and improvised on during a performance.

The first beat in a tal is called the **sam**. It is often **stressed** by the musicians.

STRUCTURE

Performances of a rag are often in **three** parts, progressing from a **slow** to **fast** tempo:

1. **Alap**
   - A **slow** introductory section
   - The notes and mood of the rag are **introduced** against a drone
   - There is **no regular pulse** and **no percussion**.

2. **Gat**
   - A **fixed composition** that is **improvised** on by the solo instrument
   - The **percussion enters**
   - A **clear pulse** is introduced.

3. **Jhalla**
   - A **fast** final section
   - The music becomes more **virtuosic** and **decorative**.

Rag Desh performed by Anoushka Shankar

Anoushka Shankar, who plays **sitar**, is the daughter of the very famous Indian musician Ravi Shankar. This version of *Rag Desh* was recorded live in 2001, at a concert in New York.

INSTRUMENTATION

1. Sitar

A **plucked string instrument** with a very long neck. It has **seven main strings**, which are used to play the melody. There are also about **12 sympathetic strings** – these aren't plucked, but resonate 'in sympathy' with the other strings, to create a characteristic shimmering sound.

2. Tabla

A **pair of drums**. The right one is called the **dayan**. It is smaller (so higher pitched) and made of wood. The left one is called the **bayan**. It is larger (so lower pitched) and made of metal. The drums are played mainly with the fingers.

RHYTHM

This version of *Rag Desh* uses **two** tals:

1. **Jhaptal** – a 10-beat cycle (2 + 3 + 2 + 3)
2. **Tintal** – a 16-beat cycle (4 + 4 + 4 + 4).

STRUCTURE

1. **Alap**
   - This section is for **sitar only**.
   - It is **slow** and has **no regular pulse**.
   - The sitar **introduces** the notes and mood of the rag.
   - The melodic line is **decorated** with slides and pitch bends (called **meends**).

2. **Gat**
   - The **tabla enters** after a few seconds.
   - The sitar plays a **fixed composition** (the 'gat') in a **moderate tempo**.
   - The sitar and tabla improvise. The **sitar's** improvisations are based on the **gat**, and the **tabla's** on the **tal**. The improvisations end with a **tihai** – a short melody or rhythm played **three** times, which ends on the **sam**.
   - Towards the end of this section, the **tempo increases**.

3. **Jhalla**
   - The music is **fast** and the sitar strings are **strummed** to create rhythmic excitement.

Mhara janam maran performed by Chiranji Lal Tanwar

This version of *Rag Desh* is a **bhajan** – a Hindu devotional song. It is performed by the Indian singer Chiranji Lal Tanwar, and was released in 2004.

INSTRUMENTATION

Chiranji Lal Tanwar is accompanied by:

1. **Sarod** – a **plucked string instrument**
2. **Sarangi** – a **bowed string instrument**
3. **Pakhawaj** – a long **drum** with a head at each end
4. **Tabla**
5. A pair of small **cymbals**.

RHYTHM

This piece uses an 8-beat cycle called **keherwa tal** (2 + 2 + 2 + 2).

STRUCTURE

1. Alap
   - The **sarangi** and then the **voice** introduce the notes of the rag.
   - The tempo is **slow** and there is **no regular pulse**.

2. Bhajan
   - The **tabla** joins in, playing in **keherwa tal**.
   - A **sung verse** is followed by **short solos** for **sarangi** and **sarod**. This pattern repeats a number of times.
   - Tanwar **decorates** important words with **melismas** and **ornaments**.

Rag Desh performed by Steve Gorn and Benjy Wertheimer

Steve Gorn (on bansuri) and Benjy Wertheimer (on esraj and tabla) are two American musicians. This version of *Rag Desh* comes from an album they released in 2004.

INSTRUMENTATION

1. **Bansuri** – a **bamboo flute** which has holes instead of keys
2. **Esraj** – a **bowed string instrument**
3. **Shruti box** – an **electronic instrument** that plays a drone
4. **Swarmandel** – a **plucked string instrument** like a zither
5. **Tabla**.

RHYTHM

This version of *Rag Desh* uses **two** tals:

1. **Rupak tal** – a 7-beat cycle (3 + 2 + 2)
2. **Ektal** – a 12-beat cycle (2 + 2 + 2 + 2 + 2 + 2).

STRUCTURE

1. **Alap**
   - This starts with the **drone** on notes D and A
   - The **bansuri** introduces the notes and mood of the rag
   - The **esraj** then takes over, before the instruments **alternate** improvised phrases
   - The tempo is **slow** and there is **no regular pulse**.

2. **Gat 1**
   - This is a **slow gat** in **rupak tal**
   - It begins with a **bansuri solo**
   - The **tabla enters** after about 30 seconds
   - The bansuri starts to play the **composed gat** shortly afterwards
   - The bansuri and tabla **improvise** around the gat and tal
   - The end of this section finishes with a **tihai**.

3. **Gat 2**
   - This is a **fast gat** in **ektal**
   - It starts with a **tabla solo**
   - The improvisation becomes more **elaborate**
   - The bansuri plays **tans** (fast scales)
   - The piece ends with three **tihais**.

Test yourself *Rag Desh*

1. *Rag Desh* is associated with which time of day and season?

    (a) early morning/winter   (b) afternoon/summer

    (c) night/spring   (d) late evening/monsoon

2. What is the name for the repeated rhythmic patterns that occur in Indian music?

3. What are sympathetic strings? Name **one** instrument that makes use of them.

4. What is a bhajan, and which version of *Rag Desh* includes one?

5. Name **two** characteristics of the alap.

6. What are tans?

7. What is the term for the composed section in a performance of a rag?

8. What is the structure of Steve Gorn and Benjy Wertheimer's version of *Rag Desh*?

9. The notes of rag desh are as below. Fill in the four blanks:

10. A tihai is often used to mark the end of a short improvisation. Briefly describe what happens in a tihai.

11. Name the **two** stringed instruments played in 'Mhara janam maran'.

12. Is Indian classical music performed from memory or from notation?

West African music and Koko

There is much diversity in West African music, from traditional call-and-response songs and complex, layered percussion music to a thriving pop scene in the cities. Through the slave trade, West African music has spread to the USA and the Caribbean, and had a notable influence on genres such as the blues, jazz and rock music.

Much traditional West African music is performed by professional musicians known as griots. Musical knowledge is passed down over the generations in each griot family by word of mouth (a process known as an **oral tradition**).

Typical features of traditional West African music are:

1. **Repetition** – rhythms, harmonies and melodies are often repeated continually to form **ostinatos**
2. **Improvisation** – melodies are frequently made up of improvised phrases
3. **Call and response** – usually occurs between a soloist (who sings or plays a phrase) and a larger group that responds with an answering phrase
4. **Layered textures** – music built up from independent lines that are designed to be heard together.

All of these features can be found in the next set work, *Yiri*, performed by a group called **Koko**. Koko is made up of six professional musicians from the country Burkina Faso.

Koko: *Yiri*

The word yiri means '**wood**', which possibly refers to the fact that all the instruments in this piece (aside from the bell) are made of wood.

The musicians performed *Yiri* **from memory**. The score was made later by notating the music heard on the recording. This type of score is called a **transcription**.

INSTRUMENTATION

The following instruments are used in *Yiri*:

1. The **balafon** – similar to a **xylophone**, this instrument is made up of **wooden bars** which are tuned to **different pitches**. **Gourds** hang beneath the bars to make the instrument sound more **resonant**.
2. The **djembe** – a **drum** shaped like a goblet, played with the **hands**.
3. The **talking drum** – a **drum** that is played with a **hooked stick** and can be used to **imitate speech** by creating different pitches and slides.

The members of Koko also **sing** (on *Yiri* they are split into a **soloist** and **chorus**).

STRUCTURE

The piece is in **three** sections:

1. **Introduction**
   - The short introduction is a **balafon solo** played using **tremolo**.
2. **Main section**
   - Throughout this section the drums play an **ostinato** and there is a **strong, clear pulse**. The music alternates between **balafon solos** and **choruses**.
   - In the middle of this section there is also a **vocal solo**, in which **call and response** is used between the **solo vocalist** and the **choir**.
3. **Coda**
   - A **short phrase** for **balafon** is played **five times** in **slightly varied** versions. The **drum ostinato** is interrupted by **rests**, and a **bell** is sounded to mark the end.

MELODY, HARMONY AND TONALITY

- *Yiri* is in the key of G♭ major. Most of the music is **hexatonic**, which means it is based on a **six-note scale** (without the note F).
- The **balafons** mostly play **short patterns**, which often **fall** from high to low. They tend to **emphasise** the notes **G♭** and **D♭** (the tonic and dominant in G♭ major).
  The balafon has solo **breaks** in between the choruses, which are more **virtuosic**.
- During the **choruses**, the group sings together in **unison**. Like the balafon, the chorus has **short, falling phrases** that **emphasise** the notes **G♭** and **D♭**.

RHYTHM, METRE AND TEMPO

- The **main metre** is $\frac{4}{4}$, although a few bars are in other metres.
- After the introduction, which is in a **free tempo**, the rest of the piece maintains a **steady pulse**.
- **Syncopation** is frequently used, especially in the vocal and balafon parts.
- During one of the vocal solos, the balafon plays semiquavers in groups of three, creating **cross rhythms**.
- The vocal soloist makes use of **triplets**.
- The drums play a **rhythmic ostinato** which lasts **throughout the piece**. It consists of a **quaver** and **two semiquavers** played over and over again. On top of this, the djembe plays occasional **fills**.

TEXTURE AND DYNAMICS

Most of *Yiri* has a **layered texture**, but it also includes:

- A **monophonic** texture in the introduction (balafon solo)
- Occasional **heterophonic** textures, created when the **two balafons** play **different versions** of the **same tune** at the **same time**.

There is **little dynamic variation** throughout the piece.

1. Which country does Koko come from?

2. Explain the following rhythmic devices that are used in *Yiri*:

    (a) cross rhythm

    (b) syncopation

    (c) triplet

3. What is the term for the repeated pattern used in the drum parts?

4. What sort of texture does the work open with?

5. What is the name for the tuned percussion instrument made from wooden bars?

6. What is the name for the phrase structure, used in *Yiri*, in which a melody for solo singer is answered by the chorus?

7. What instrumental technique is used in the introduction?

8. Most of the melodies in *Yiri* are built from a scale of six notes. What is the term for this sort of scale?

9. Apart from talking drums, name one other type of drum played on *Yiri*.

10. Describe two characteristics of the melodies in this piece.

11. 'Yiri' means 'wood'. Why might this be an appropriate title for the piece?

The listening paper (Unit 3)

The listening paper lasts for one-and-a-half hours and is worth 40% of the total marks for GCSE Music. It is divided into two sections.

In **Section A** you have to answer questions on extracts from eight of the 12 set works you have studied. Each extract will be played several times on CD as you answer the questions, but you won't have scores of the extracts in the exam. Section A accounts for 68 of the total 80 marks available for Unit 3 and you have to answer the questions on all eight extracts – there will not be any choice.

Most of these questions will be about specific features of the set works and will require short (often one-word) answers. However, you should also expect a few more general questions related to the extract – for example, asking you to name three important features of the Baroque style. There will also be a few questions in which you will be expected to show your understanding of music notation by completing some gaps in a short rhythm, melody or chord progression from the extract. Some students find this type of question particularly difficult, but there is plenty of help in the *Edexcel GCSE Music Listening Tests* from Rhinegold Education.

In **Section B** you will have to answer one question (from a choice of two) that will probably focus on one set work, although it could ask you to compare certain features of two or more set works. The question is likely to be divided into several parts, the first of which will probably ask a few simple facts about the context of the work – such as when it was written or where it might be performed. The main question in Section B will ask you to discuss a number of musical elements in the work(s) concerned. This question attracts 10 marks and will require a relatively long answer. You will not be played any musical extracts for this question, nor will you have access to the score(s). The questions in Section B, which must be completed in 25 minutes, account for the remaining 12 marks for Unit 3.

In the rest of this book we will look at what is meant by the elements of music and consider what type of detail you could include in your answers. Remember that in the exam the question will ask you to discuss a number of elements in the work(s) concerned – not just one – and that the quality of your written communication will be assessed. For a good mark, set out your answer clearly (perhaps by devoting a short paragraph to each element). Use correct musical terms wherever you can and support your answers by giving *specific* locations of the points you make (e.g. by stating that Bernstein uses cross rhythm *in the accompaniment* at the *start* of 'Something's Coming').

The elements of music

Success in the exam is partly dependent on your understanding of the elements of music (melody, harmony and so on) through your knowledge of the set works. There are two parts to the exam. **Section A** mostly involves short questions, multiple choice and brief notation exercises. In **Section B** you will have to write a longer answer to a more detailed question on one of the set works (or possibly on a comparison of two set works). Your understanding of the elements of music will mostly be tested in Section B.

Edexcel gives as an example of a longer Section B question: 'Comment on how Schoenberg uses the following musical elements in *Peripetie*: tonality and harmony; instruments and texture; melody; dynamics and tempo; structure' (10 marks).

To achieve full marks for a question like this, you will need to make a total of **ten valid points**: roughly two points for each of the five parts in the question (although the quality of your written English will also affect your mark). Although eight elements are referred to in this particular question, some Section B questions may ask you to comment on just five elements, so it is a good idea to learn at least **two points** about each element of music in each set work. Remember that some elements of music are more important in some works than others (for instance harmony is more important in Mozart's symphony than in *Rag Desh*), so base your revision around what is listed in this guide. The following section explains what you need to know about each element and how you will be tested on it in the exam.

METRE

The metre of a piece tells us how the beats are grouped in the music, and is indicated by a **time signature**.

The terms 'duple', 'triple' and quadruple' refer to how many main beats there are in each bar:

- **Duple**: **two** main beats in a bar (e.g. sections of Bernstein are in $\frac{2}{4}$)
- **Triple**: **three** main beats in a bar (e.g. the main metre of Reich is $\frac{3}{2}$)
- **Quadruple**: **four** main beats in a bar (e.g. Buckley is in $\frac{12}{8}$).

You can also use the words 'simple' and 'compound' to indicate how the main beat is divided:

- **Simple**: each beat divides into **two** – the upper number of the time signature is 2, 3 or 4 (e.g. Mozart in $\frac{4}{4}$)
- **Compound**: each beat divides into **three** – the upper number of the time signature is 6, 9 or 12 (e.g. Davis in $\frac{6}{4}$).

Some music has no fixed pattern of beats and is in a **free metre**, such as the opening of Anoushka Shankar's performance of *Rag Desh*. You should also point out if the metre changes frequently, such as towards the end of *Electric Counterpoint*.

EXAMPLE SECTION A QUESTIONS

1. What is the metre of this extract?
2. Is this extract in a simple or compound metre?
3. This extract starts in $\frac{4}{4}$. What does the time signature change to later in the extract?

SECTION B QUESTIONS

In Section B, you are likely to be asked about metre in conjunction with rhythm. Answers on metre can be very short: just remember to describe the metre and to say whether it changes in the piece (and, if so, where).

TEST YOURSELF

1. State whether each of the following metres is (i) duple, triple or quadruple, **and** (ii) simple or compound:

   (a) $\frac{3}{4}$ (b) $\frac{12}{8}$ (c) $\frac{4}{4}$ (d) $\frac{3}{2}$

2. What is the term for a metre with no fixed beat pattern?

TEMPO

The tempo describes the **speed** of the music – how fast or slow it goes. It can be described in **words** (e.g. 'allegro' or 'sehr rasch'), or as a **metronome mark** (e.g. $\quarternote$ = 176).

In questions on tempo, you should also mention whether the speed changes (e.g. Chopin's prelude makes use of rubato and slows down with a ritenuto in the last two bars).

EXAMPLE SECTION A QUESTIONS

1. Describe the tempo of this piece.
2. What does the term 'ritenuto' mean?
3. Which of the following terms best describes the tempo of this extract: adagio, molto allegro or prestissimo?

SECTION B QUESTIONS

In Section B, you may be asked to comment on tempo in works which include tempo changes, such as Schoenberg or Chopin. Most of the set works don't have tempo changes and you are less likely to be asked about these. For an example question on rhythm and tempo, see the 'rhythm' section below.

TEST YOURSELF

1. What is the term used for the fluctuations of tempo that occur in performances of Chopin's Prelude No. 15?

2. What does the tempo marking ♩ = 122 mean?

3. What do the terms (i) 'adagio' and (ii) 'allegro' mean?

RHYTHM

When you write about rhythm in the exam, you might want to mention:

- Rhythms that **characterise** a melody (e.g. dotted rhythms in the opening melody of Chopin)
- **Repeated** rhythmic patterns (e.g. the ♩♫ ostinato in *Yiri*)
- Whether rhythms are **complex and varied** or **simple and repetitive**
- **Contrasts** of rhythm (e.g. slow- and fast-moving rhythms in Schoenberg).

You should also be prepared to write about rhythmic devices, such as:

- **Syncopation** (e.g.in Reich)
- **Cross rhythms** (e.g. in Bernstein)
- **Hemiolas** (e.g. in Handel)
- **Swung rhythms** (e.g. in Davis)
- **Triplets** (e.g. in *Yiri*)
- **Anacrusis** (e.g. in Mozart).

EXAMPLE SECTION A QUESTIONS

1. Complete the missing rhythm.
2. Name the rhythmic device that occurs in the third bar of the extract.
3. In the opening passage the pianist plays a septuplet. What is a septuplet?

EXAMPLE SECTION B QUESTIONS

'Comment on the use of rhythm and tempo in the performance of *Rag Desh* by Anoushka Shankar.'

Points you could make might include:

- This piece starts with an alap, in which the tempo is free and the rhythms are improvised
- The second section is a gat, in which a tal is introduced: this is in a fixed metre, with a steady tempo
- The tal is repeated on the tabla, with constant variation around its basic rhythm
- In the third section the tempo is quicker and there is more rhythmic activity.

TEST YOURSELF

1. What is meant by the term 'syncopation'?

2. What is the term for the rhythmic device where two bars of $\frac{3}{4}$ sound like three bars of $\frac{2}{4}$?

3. In which style of music do swung rhythms frequently occur?

MELODY

Questions on melody might ask you to describe the **shape** of a melody or the **scale** it's based on, and to identify any **melodic devices** used (such as imitation or inversion). Some of the words you could use to describe a melody are:

- **Diatonic** (e.g. Handel) or **atonal** (e.g. Schoenberg)
- **Pentatonic** (e.g. *Skye Waulking Song*) or **hexatonic** (e.g. *Yiri*)
- **Sustained** and **lyrical** (e.g. Chopin)
- **Short** and **fragmented** (e.g. Schoenberg)
- **Conjunct** (e.g. second subject of Mozart) or **disjunct** (e.g. Schoenberg).

You could also mention if a melody contains:

- **Ornamentation** (e.g. Chopin)
- **Blue notes** (e.g. Davis)
- **Scalic passages** (e.g. Mozart)
- **Sequences** (e.g. Handel)
- **Motivic repetition** (e.g. Reich).

Think about the material that makes up the melody, and how it is developed throughout the piece.

EXAMPLE SECTION A QUESTIONS

1. Is the melody of this extract conjunct or disjunct?
2. Complete the missing notes of the given melody.
3. On which scale is the melody based?
4. Which **one** of the following best describes the melodic device used in bars 4–10 of the extract?
   (a) imitation   (b) inversion   (c) question and answer   (d) sequence

EXAMPLE SECTION B QUESTION

'Comment on the use of melody in 'Why Does My Heart Feel So Bad?' by Moby.'

Points you could make might include:

- The vocal melody consists of two samples taken from a 1950s gospel choir recording
- The samples are one or two bars in length
- They aren't developed but are repeated through looping
- These melodies have a narrow range
- Other melodies used (such as the string-synth countermelody) have a similarly narrow range.

TEST YOURSELF

1. If a melody contains frequent wide leaps, is it conjunct or disjunct?

2. What is the term for a melodic phrase that is immediately repeated at a different pitch?

3. What are blue notes?

THE ELEMENTS OF MUSIC

HARMONY

'Harmony' means anything to do with chords and chord progressions. For a question on harmony, you can talk about the type of chords used in a piece and how fast they change (the harmonic rhythm).

The general harmonic language:

- Can be mostly **consonant** (e.g. Handel)
- Or mostly **dissonant** (e.g. Schoenberg)
- Can use **simple diatonic harmonies** (e.g. Moby)
- Or can include some **chromaticism** and **dissonance** (e.g. Chopin and Buckley).

Other **harmonic features** you could mention include:

- **Pedal notes** (e.g. Chopin)
- **Cadences** (e.g. the plagal cadence at the end of Handel)
- Chords moving in **parallel motion** (e.g. Buckley)
- **Added-note chords** (e.g. Bernstein)
- **Circle of 5ths progression** (e.g. Mozart).

EXAMPLE SECTION A QUESTIONS

1. Complete the missing chords in the chord sequence.
2. Write out the notes of a G⁷ chord.
3. This extract is diatonic: what does that mean?
4. What type of cadence does this extract end with?

EXAMPLE SECTION B QUESTIONS

'Comment on the use of harmony in *Skye Waulking Song*.'

Points you could make might include:

- The three main chords used in the song are G, Em and C
- The harmony is entirely diatonic
- Because the dominant chord isn't used, the music feels modal
- The ending contains repeated plagal cadences.

1. What is meant by 'harmonic rhythm'?

2. In the key of G major, name the cadence created by each of these chord progressions (Roman numerals are given in brackets).

    (a) C–G (IV–I)   (b) D–G (V–I)   (c) G–D (I–V)

3. What is the correct term for a note that is repeated in the bass, while the harmonies above it change?

TONALITY

'Tonality' refers to the key(s) of the music. In the exam, questions on tonality could include:

- The **key** a piece is in (e.g. the Handel is in A major)
- The keys a piece **modulates** to, and how these keys are related to the tonic (e.g. Chopin modulates to C♯ minor, the tonic minor)
- How the use of different keys helps to **define the structure** (e.g. in Mozart, the second subject is in the relative major in the exposition, but in the tonic in the recapitulation)
- Whether the music is **tonal**, **modal** or **atonal** (e.g. Handel is tonal, Davis is modal and Schoenberg is atonal)
- The use of certain **scales** (e.g. *Skye Waulking Song* uses the pentatonic scale).

EXAMPLE SECTION A QUESTIONS

1. What is the key of this extract?
2. Which word best describes the tonality of this piece?
    (a) atonal   (b) modal   (c) tonal
3. This extract starts in E major. In what key does it end?

EXAMPLE SECTION B QUESTION

'Comment on the use of tonality in Chopin's Prelude No. 15.'

Points you could mention might include the following:

- It is in Db major, with a central section in the enharmonic tonic minor, C# minor
- This tonal structure helps to reinforce the ABA structure of the movement, as the key changes coincide with changes in the main material
- The first A section and the B section both modulate to related keys for a few bars.

TEST YOURSELF

1. What does 'modulation' mean?

2. If the tonic key of a piece is G minor, how would you describe the key of Bb major in relation to the tonic?

   (a) the dominant   (b) the relative major   (c) the tonic major

3. How many notes do (i) pentatonic and (ii) hexatonic scales have?

TEXTURE

Texture refers to the simultaneous lines in a piece of music – how many there are and how they interact with each other.

Textures might be:

- **Monophonic** (e.g. the opening of *Yiri*)
- **Polyphonic** or **contrapuntal** (e.g. Reich)
- **Homophonic** (e.g. Chopin).

They may also include:

- **Countermelodies** (e.g. *Skye Waulking Song*)
- **Drones** (e.g. *Rag Desh*) or **pedals** (e.g. Chopin)
- **Block chords** (e.g. Mozart)
- **Broken chords** (e.g. Chopin)
- **Dialogue** and **imitation** (e.g. Mozart)
- **Canons** (e.g. Reich).

Remember that **general points** about texture are also valid, such as:

- Whether a texture is thick or thin
- How often the texture changes
- How many independent parts the texture contains.

EXAMPLE SECTION A QUESTIONS

1. In one word, describe the texture in the opening of this piece.
2. At the start of this extract, there are repeated G♯ quavers above the melody. What is the correct musical term for this device?
3. How does the texture in this extract change?

EXAMPLE SECTION B QUESTION

'Comment on the texture of Mozart's Symphony No. 40 (first movement).'

Points you could make might include:

- It is mostly homophonic, with occasional monophonic and contrapuntal passages
- Dialogue occurs between the strings and woodwind at the start of the second subject
- Octave doublings are often used
- There are frequent contrasts between different types of texture (thin versus thick).

TEST YOURSELF

1. Match each definition with the correct word:

   (i) an unaccompanied melodic line
   (ii) a tune with accompaniment
   (iii) two or more simultaneous melodies
   (iv) different parts added on top of one another

   (a) a homophonic texture   (b) a layered texture

   (c) a contrapuntal texture   (d) a monophonic texture

STRUCTURE

This refers to the **overall form** of a movement or piece of music. You can also break this down to talk about the role of **individual sections** within a movement, and consider the **phrase structure** of the melody.

The **overall structure** of a piece can be:

1. A **standard form**, for example:

   - Ternary form (Chopin)
   - Sonata form (Mozart)
   - Verse-chorus form (Buckley and Moby).

2. A **non-standard form**, which will need to be described, for example:

   - *Yiri*: there is a short introduction (a balafon solo) followed by the main section, which alternates between balafon solos and choruses. In the middle of this section there is a vocal solo. A coda ends the piece.

The overall structure of a piece can be broken down into **shorter sections**, which may have their own specific names, for example:

   - Mozart: exposition (first and second subject), development and recapitulation
   - *Rag Desh*: alap, gat and jhalla
   - Buckley: intro, verse, chorus and bridge sections.

Most of the set works will contain one or more of the following types of section:

   - A section where ideas are **introduced** (e.g. intro in Buckley)
   - A section where the **main idea** is presented (e.g. first subject of Mozart)
   - Sections where **contrasting ideas** are presented (e.g. 'B' section of Chopin)
   - One or more sections where ideas are **developed** (e.g. solo sections of Davis)
   - Sections where ideas are **brought back** (e.g. the male vocal sample in Moby)
   - A section used to **end a piece** (e.g. the coda in *Yiri*).

The **phrase structure** of a piece may contain:

   - **Call-and-response** passages (*Skye Waulking Song*)
   - **Question-and-answer** phrases (Mozart)
   - The alternation of **polyphonic** and **homophonic** passages (Handel)
   - A **12-bar blues** structure (Davis)
   - Regular **four-bar phrases** (Moby).

EXAMPLE SECTION A QUESTIONS

1. This movement is in sonata form. Give the correct term for the sub-section from which this extract comes.
2. What type of arrangement is this piece?
   (a) head arrangement   (b) riff arrangement   (c) verse-chorus arrangement
3. This piece could be described as being in ABA form. What is another name for this form?
   (a) binary form   (b) rondo form   (c) ternary form

EXAMPLE SECTION B QUESTION

'Comment on the structure of Mozart's Symphony No. 40 (first movement).'

Points you could make might include two or more of the following:

- It is in sonata form
- It contains an exposition, development section and recapitulation
- The exposition has a first and second subject
- The first subject is in the tonic in both the exposition and recapitulation; the second subject is in the relative major in the exposition and the tonic in the recapitulation
- The development section develops material from the exposition and passes through various keys
- The movement uses question-and-answer phrases.

TEST YOURSELF

1. What is the term used for when a phrase sung by a soloist is answered by a phrase sung by several people?

2. Whereabouts would the following sections be found in a piece of music: at the beginning, in the middle, or at the end?

   (a) alap   (b) the 'B' section of ternary form   (c) bridge

   (d) coda   (e) breakdown   (f) exposition

In the exam you will come across questions on how instruments, voices and technology are used. They may include the choice of instruments used in a piece, the roles that they play and the timbres they produce.

Instruments or groups of instruments may have one or more of these roles:

- Playing **melodic** material (e.g. the frontline instruments in Davis)
- Playing **harmonic** material (e.g. the piano in Moby)
- Playing **rhythmic** material (e.g. the drum kit in Buckley)
- **Doubling** other forces (e.g. the string parts doubling the voices in Handel)
- Playing an **independent line** within a contrapuntal texture (e.g. the guitar parts in the first section of Reich)
- Engaging in **dialogue** with other instruments (e.g. strings and wind instruments in the second subject of Mozart).

Timbre refers to the different sounds that each instrument can produce, for example:

- String instruments can be **bowed** or **plucked**
- Brass can play **with a mute** to create a softer, thinner tone
- Guitars can be **strummed** or **finger-picked**.

If you are asked how the voices are used in an extract, you could mention:

- The **role** of the singers (e.g. a solo singer is answered by a group of singers in *Yiri*)
- How the vocal lines are used to bring out the **meaning** of certain words (e.g. Buckley)
- Whether the vocal line is **high** or **low** in a singer's register, and whether it covers a **wide range** or a **narrow range** of pitches
- Whether the word setting is **syllabic** or **melismatic**.

For a question on music technology, you might be expected to write about:

- The use of **electronic instruments** (such as synthesisers or drum machines)
- The use of **samples** (e.g. the vocal samples in Moby)
- The use of technology to **build up** a track (e.g. through multi-tracking and sequencing)
- The use of **digital effects** such as reverb or delay.

EXAMPLE SECTION A QUESTIONS

1.   Which instrument is playing the melody in this extract?
2.   Mozart's orchestra uses a string section. Name two instruments (other than violins) that can be found in an orchestral string section.
3.   Name two folk music instruments that are used in this piece.
4.   What digital effect has been applied to the melody at the end of this extract?

EXAMPLE SECTION B QUESTION

'Comment on Schoenberg's use of instruments in *Peripetie*.'

Points you could make might include:

- Schoenberg writes for a very large symphony orchestra made up of strings, woodwind, and large brass and percussion sections
- He uses more unusual orchestral instruments such as contrabassoon, cor anglais, piccolo and tam-tam
- He uses extremes of range (e.g. very low and high horn parts)
- He uses many unusual instrumental timbres (e.g. muted horns, tremolo double basses, bowed cymbal)
- He includes many sudden changes of instrumentation
- His use of the orchestra is designed to produce the maximum expressive impact typical of the Expressionist style.

TEST YOURSELF

1.   Name **four** woodwind instruments often used in orchestras

2.   Name **two** instrumental techniques that could be used on a cello

3.   With which set works would you associate the following instruments and timbres?

     (a) balafon   (b) bouzouki   (c) solo piano

     (d) trumpet with a mute   (e) vocal chorus

DYNAMICS

'Dynamics' is another word for volume: how loud or soft the music is, and how quickly or suddenly the volume changes.

Here are a few examples of how dynamics are used in the set works:

- **Terraced dynamics** (Handel)
- Sudden, **violent contrasts**, ranging from ***ppp*** to ***fff*** (Schoenberg)
- **Detailed dynamic markings**, incorporating **subtle changes** with many **crescendos** and **diminuendos** (Chopin)
- **Little dynamic contrast** (*Yiri*).

EXAMPLE SECTION A QUESTIONS

1. What is the Italian term for the symbol ⬅ ?
2. Does the first movement of Mozart's Symphony No. 40 begin quietly or loudly?

EXAMPLE SECTION B QUESTION

'Comment on the use of dynamics in Schoenberg's *Peripetie*.'

Points you could make might include two or more of the following:

- **Extremes** of dynamics are used: from ***ppp*** to ***fff***
- There are **sudden dynamic contrasts**
- The dynamics are very **detailed**: each entry has a dynamic marking and there is frequent use of crescendo and diminuendo markings.

TEST YOURSELF

1. What does the term 'sotto voce' mean?

2. Arrange the following dynamic markings in order of loudness, from quietest to loudest:

    (a) *f*　　　　　(b) *mf*　　　　　(c) *pp*

    (d) *fff*　　　　　(e) *mp*　　　　　(f) *mp*

Glossary

Accent. Emphasis on a note or chord (sometimes indicated by the symbol >).

Acciaccatura. A very short ornamental note played just before a principal melodic note.

Added-note chord. A chord which includes one or more non-standard notes, such as a 2nd or 6th above the root.

Alto. A low female or high male voice.

Anacrusis. An upbeat. An accented note or group of notes that come before the first strong beat of a phrase.

Atonal. Music that avoids keys or modes, i.e. no one pitch stands out consistently in the way that the tonic does in tonal music.

Balafon. An instrument from West Africa similar to a xylophone.

Balanced phrases. Phrases of the same length paired together, so that the first sounds like a question that is answered by the second phrase. See **question and answer**.

Bass. (1) The lowest male voice. (2) The lowest-pitched line in a piece of music, on which the harmonies are based.

Beat. The beat in a piece of music is a regular pulse that we can clap along to. The number of beats in each bar is indicated by the **time signature**.

Blue note. A note (usually the third, fifth or seventh degree of a major scale) performed at a slightly lower pitch than normal for expressive effect.

Blues. A style of music created by the rural African-American population in the southern states of America during the early 20th century.

Break. In jazz and pop music, a short instrumental solo.

Bridge. In jazz and pop music, a contrasting passage that connects two longer sections.

Broken chord. A chord in which the notes are played one after the other rather than at the same time.

Cadence. Formed by the last two chords of a phrase, a type of musical punctuation. See **imperfect cadence**, **perfect cadence** and **plagal cadence**.

Call and response. A pair of phrases, performed by different musicians, in which the second phrase is heard as a reply to the first. This term normally refers to jazz, pop and world music.

Canon. A musical structure in which the melody in one part is repeated exactly by other parts, while the original part continues with different music.

Chorus. (1) The repeated refrain in a verse-chorus structure. (2) A movement for whole choir in a large-scale choral work (such as an oratorio). (3) One statement of the 12-bar blues progression.

Chromatic notes. Notes that don't belong to the scale of the key the music is currently in. For example, B♮ and D♯ are chromatic notes in the key of F major. Opposite of **diatonic notes**.

Circle of 5ths. A harmonic progression in which the root of each succeeding chord is a 5th lower (or a 4th higher) than the previous one.

Clef. A symbol placed at the beginning of a line of music that defines what the pitches of the notes are.

Coda. A section of music that ends a piece.

Compound time. A metre in which the main beat is sub-divided into three equal portions (e.g. a dotted-crotchet beat divided into three quavers). Opposite of **simple time**.

Conjunct. A conjunct melody moves by step (i.e., in major or minor seconds) rather than by larger intervals. Opposite of **disjunct**.

Consonance. Notes that are consonant sound pleasing when played together. Opposite of **dissonance**.

Continuo. An accompanying part in instrumental music of the Baroque period. The continuo is played by a bass instrument (such as cello) and a harmony instrument (such as harpsichord).

Contrapuntal. Adjective to describe music that uses **counterpoint**.

Countermelody. A second melody in a piece that is heard at the same time as the main melody, to provide contrast.

Counterpoint. A texture in which two or more melodic lines, each one significant in itself, are played together at the same time.

Crescendo. A gradual increase in dynamic. The opposite of **diminuendo**.

Cross rhythm. The presence in a passage of music of conflicting rhythms (e.g. groups of three notes played in one line while groups of two are played simultaneously in another).

Delay. An audio effect that can be electronically added to music to give the effect of an echo.

Dialogue. When two or more instruments or voices have a musical 'conversation', with the individual parts responding to one another with different ideas and phrases.

Diatonic notes. Notes that belong to the scale of the key the music is currently in. For example, B♭ and D are diatonic notes in the key of F major. Opposite of **chromatic notes**.

Diminuendo. A gradual decrease in dynamic. Opposite of **crescendo**.

Disjunct. A disjunct melody moves by leaps, or intervals larger than a 2nd. Opposite of **conjunct**.

Dissonance. Notes that are dissonant produce a clashing sound when played together. Opposite of **consonance**.

Distortion. A digital effect that alters the sound of an instrument so that it becomes rougher and harsher.

Dominant. The fifth note of a scale. For example, C is the dominant of F.

Dorian mode. A scale that uses the following pattern of tones (T) and semitones (s): T–s–T–T–T–s–T. Starting on D, it consists of all of the white notes on a keyboard: D–E–F–G–A–B–C–D.

Dotted rhythm. A rhythm that contains pairs of notes in the pattern long–short. The first note is dotted and the second is a third of the dotted note's value (e.g. dotted crotchet–quaver).

Doubling. A note or passage in one part is played by another part at the same time, either at the same **pitch** or at a different **octave**.

Drone. A sustained note that is held in one part while other parts play or sing melodies against it.

Drum machine. An electronic device that replicates the sounds of various percussion instruments.

Dynamics. How loudly or softly the music is played; the volume of the music.

Enharmonic. The same pitch notated in two different ways. For example, A♯ and B♭.

EQ. Short for 'equalisation'. Process of adjusting the relative level of frequencies in an audio signal.

Falsetto. A vocal technique used by men to sing notes higher than those within their normal voice range.

Fill. A short passage of music between two sections of a melody.

Flanging. A digital effect that combines two copies of the same signal, with the second delayed slightly, to produce a swirling, sweeping effect.

Free tempo. Describes music without a regular pulse.

Genre. A type of music or musical form, such as the symphony or sacred choral music.

Gospel. A type of vocal music that expresses Christian beliefs.

Harmonic rhythm. How often the harmony changes in a passage of music.

Harpsichord. The most common keyboard instrument of the Baroque period. Similar to the piano, except that the strings are plucked rather than hit.

Hemiola. A rhythmic device in which two bars of $\frac{3}{4}$ sound like three bars of $\frac{2}{4}$.

Heterophonic. A texture in which different versions of the same melody are heard simultaneously.

Hexachord. A chord made up of six notes.

Hexatonic scale. A scale made up of six notes.

Homophonic. A texture in which one part has the melody and the other parts accompany.

Imitation. A melodic idea in one part is immediately copied by another part, often at a different pitch, while the first part continues with other music.

Imperfect cadence. A cadence consisting of any chord – usually I, ii or IV – followed by the dominant (V).

Improvisation. The process, most common in jazz, of spontaneously creating new music as you perform.

Instrumentation. The choice of instruments for a piece of music.

Interval. The distance between two notes. For example, the interval between the notes F and A is a 3rd (A is the third note of the F major scale).

Inversion. When a melody is inverted, the intervals between the notes are turned upside down. E.g. a rising 5th (D to A) becomes a falling 5th (D to G).

Key. The key indicates the scale that a section or piece of music is based on. For example, music in the key of G major uses notes of the G major scale.

Lament. A poem or piece of music that expresses grief.

Layered. A texture made up of independent lines which are designed to be heard together.

Legato. Smooth playing, without gaps between the notes. May be indicated by slurs or phrase marks.

Loop. A short segment of music that is repeated a number of times in succession.

Melisma. One syllable sung to several notes.

Metre. The metre refers to the pulse of the music and is indicated by the **time signature**.

Metronome mark. An indication of how fast to play a piece by specifying how many beats per minute there should be. E.g. a metronome mark of ♩ = 60 means that there are 60 crotchet beats per minute, or one crotchet beat per second.

Mixolydian mode. A scale that uses the following pattern of tones (T) and semitones (s): T–T–s–T–T–s–T. Starting on G, it consists of all of the white notes on a keyboard: G–A–B–C–D–E–F–G.

Mode. Different types of seven-note scales, other than the major and minor. See **Dorian mode** and **Mixolydian mode**.

Modulation. (1) The process of changing key in a passage of music. (2) A digital effect that makes the music fluctuate in pitch slightly.

Monophonic. A texture that consists of only one melodic line.

Motif. A short but distinctive musical idea that can be changed in various ways in order to create a longer passage of music.

Mute. A device that can be fitted to an instrument to quieten the sound.

Octave. An interval formed from two notes that are 12 semitones apart. Both notes have the same name.

Ornaments. Small musical additions that decorate a melody. See **acciaccatura**, **turn** and **trill**.

Ostinato. A repeating melodic, harmonic or rhythmic motif, heard continuously throughout part or the whole of a piece.

Overdubbing. Recording a new part over the top of existing material.

Panning. Used in stereo recordings to control where the sound is coming from. Sounds can be panned to the left or right, or placed in the centre.

Parallel motion. Movement of two or more parts in the same direction, with the interval between them remaining essentially the same.

Pedal note. A sustained or continuously repeated pitch, often in the bass, that is heard against changing harmonies. When a pedal is **inverted**, it is heard in the middle or top of the texture.

Perfect cadence. A cadence consisting of the dominant chord followed by the tonic (V–I).

Pentatonic scale. A scale made up of five notes.

Pitch. How high or low a note sounds. For example, in an ascending scale the pitch of the music rises, and notes lower down on the stave have a lower pitch.

Pitch bend. A short slide up or down to a main note.

Pizzicato. A direction to pluck notes on a string instrument.

Plagal cadence. A cadence consisting of the subdominant chord followed by the tonic (IV–I).

Polyphony. A texture in which two or more melodic lines, each one significant in itself, are played together at the same time.

Prelude. A short piece of music that often acts as an introduction to a longer work, although it can also stand by itself.

Pulse. A regularly recurring sense of **beat** common to most styles of music.

Question and answer. A pair of phrases in which the second one is heard as a reply to the first.

Range. The notes that a singer or instrumentalist can sing or play.

Register. A part of the **range** of an instrument or voice.

Relative major, relative minor. Keys that have the same **key signature** but a different **tonic**. The tonic of a relative minor is three semitones below the tonic of its relative major (e.g. C major and A minor).

Reverb. An effect used to alter music so that it sounds as if it was recorded in a reverberant, echoey space.

Riff. A short, catchy melodic or rhythmic idea that is repeated throughout a jazz or pop song.

Rondo. A musical structure in which a main melody alternates with contrasting sections (ABACADA).

Sample. A short section from a recorded audio track that can be digitally manipulated and altered for insertion into a new track.

Sampler. An electronic device, like a synthesiser, that allows the user to alter and manipulate musical **samples**.

Scale. A sequence of notes that move by step either upwards or downwards. Different types of scales have different patterns of **intervals**.

Semitone. Half of a tone. The smallest interval in Western music in general use.

Sequence. Immediate repetition of a melodic or harmonic idea at a different pitch, or a succession of different pitches.

Sequencer. An electronic device or piece of computer software that allows the user to create and edit MIDI and audio files.

Serial. Atonal music that uses a predetermined series of the 12 chromatic notes to guarantee equality of all pitches.

Seventh chord. A chord made up of a triad and a note a 7th above the root.

Simple time. A metre in which the main beat is sub-divided into two equal portions (e.g. a crotchet beat divided into two quavers). Opposite of **compound time**.

Soprano. The highest female voice.

Supertonic. The second degree of a diatonic scale.

Sustaining pedal. The right-hand pedal on a piano, which when pressed causes the notes to still sound even after the keys have been released.

Swung rhythm. In jazz and the blues, a relaxing of strict quaver rhythm, so that ♪ ♪ is played as $\overset{3}{\overline{}}$ ♩ ♪ or even ♩. ♪ , depending on the speed and mood of the piece.

Syllabic. Vocal music that has one note to each syllable.

Symphony. A type of composition for orchestra, usually in four movements.

Syncopation. Placing the accents in parts of the bar that are not normally emphasised, such as on weak beats or between beats.

Synthesiser. An electronic device with a keyboard that allows the player to add digital effects and to manipulate the sounds produced.

Tab. A method of notation for plucked instruments such as the lute and guitar, in which the pitches of the notes are indicated by their fingering.

Tempo. The speed of the music.

Tenor. A high male voice.

Ternary form. A musical structure of three sections. The outer sections are similar and the central one contrasting (ABA).

Texture. The relationship between the various simultaneous lines in a passage of music, dependent on such features as the number and function of the parts and the spacing between them.

Timbre. The element of music concerned with the actual sound quality, or tone colour, of the music.

Time signature. Two numbers (for example $\frac{2}{4}$ or $\frac{6}{8}$) at the start of a stave that indicate the metre of the music. The bottom number indicates the type of beat (such as crotchet or quaver) and the top number shows how many of those beats are in each bar.

Tonality. The use of major and minor keys in music and the ways in which these keys are related.

Tonic. The starting note of a major or minor scale, and the note from which a key takes its name. E.g. F is the tonic of F major.

Tremolo. A musical effect that refers to a very quick and continuous repetition of a single note (on bowed or plucked string instruments) or of two alternating notes (on keyboard instruments).

Triad. A chord of three notes: a bass note and notes a 3rd and 5th above it.

Trill. An ornament consisting of a rapid alternation of two adjacent pitches.

Triplet. A group of three equal notes played in the time normally taken by two of the same type.

Turn. A four-note ornament that 'turns' around the main note. It starts on the note above, drops to the main note, drops to the note below and then returns to the main note.

Unison. Simultaneous performance of the same pitch or pitches by more than one person.

Verse. A section in a song that usually has lyrics unique to that section (they tend to change for each verse).

Verse-chorus form. A type of popular song in which, in its most basic structure, the **verses** are interspersed with a repeated **chorus**.

Virtuoso. A highly-skilled singer or instrumentalist, capable of performing technically difficult music.

Word painting. The use of musical devices and features to illustrate and highlight specific words in the lyrics.